Missing Lives

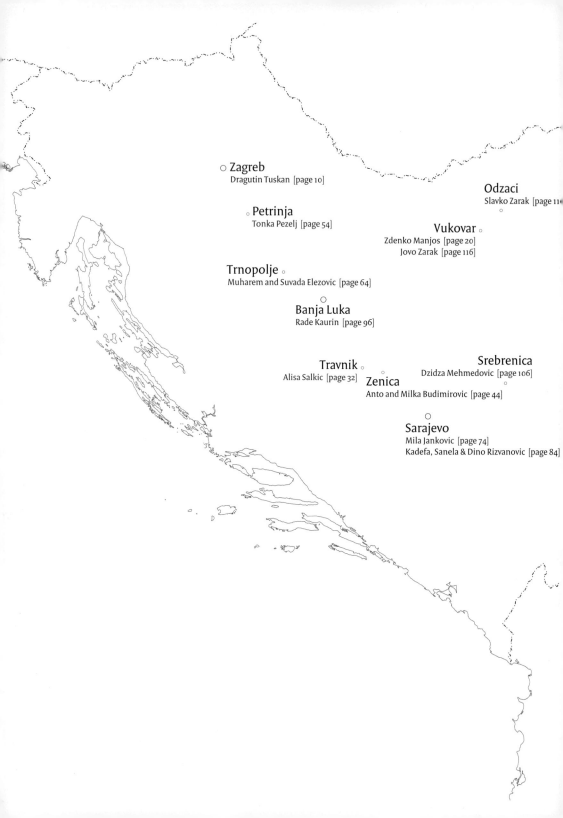

Zagreb
Dragutin Tuskan [page 10]

Odzaci
Slavko Zarak [page 11]

Petrinja
Tonka Pezelj [page 54]

Vukovar
Zdenko Manjos [page 20]
Jovo Zarak [page 116]

Trnopolje
Muharem and Suvada Elezovic [page 64]

Banja Luka
Rade Kaurin [page 96]

Travnik
Alisa Salkic [page 32]

Srebrenica
Dzidza Mehmedovic [page 106]

Zenica
Anto and Milka Budimirovic [page 44]

Sarajevo
Mila Jankovic [page 74]
Kadefa, Sanela & Dino Rizvanovic [page 84]

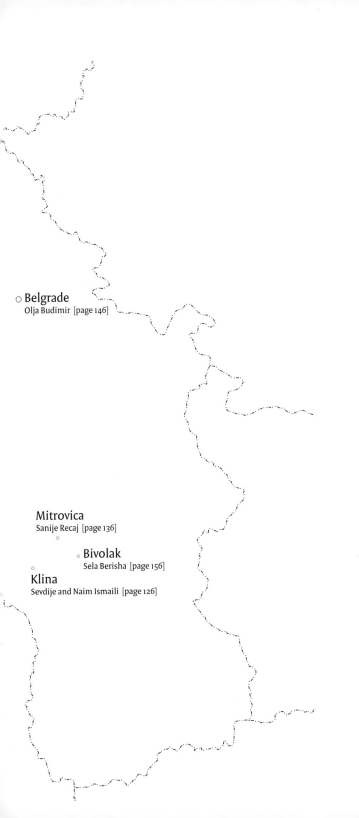

○ Belgrade
Olja Budimir [page 146]

Mitrovica
Sanije Recaj [page 136]
○

○ Bivolak
Sela Berisha [page 156]
○
Klina
Sevdije and Naim Ismaili [page 126]

4   Published in 2010 by
Dewi Lewis Publishing
8 Broomfield Road, Heaton Moor,
Stockport SK4 4ND
United Kingdom

in association with

ICRC

ISBN: 978–1–904587–87–3

Designed by Mark Thomson
Edited by Paul-Henri Arni, ICRC
Printed by die Keure, Belgium

Missing Lives

Photographs by Nick Danziger
Text by Rory MacLean

Dewi Lewis Publishing · 2010

'People are not needles. They cannot vanish for ever.'

Nineteen years ago Yugoslavia died, its federation of republics con-
suming themselves in fires of ethnic and religious hatred ignited
by ruthless politicians. In ten years of successive conflicts, acts of
barbarism unseen in Europe since the Second World War were committed in horrendous numbers. As many as 140,000 people were
killed, a quarter of whom simply vanished. This shocking propor-
tion of missing lives needs to be explained.

In most cases the fathers and sons led away at gunpoint were
murdered. Governments, armies and militias worked together to
eradicate minorities, masking their actions behind the iniquitous
euphemism 'ethnic cleansing'. Their methods varied in scale but
the objective was the same across most front lines: gain territory
through the deportation, imprisonment and execution of civilians.
Making people disappear was part of military strategy.

Since 1991 the International Committee of the Red Cross in the
Balkans has been asked by families to trace 34,389 missing persons.
Every single one of them left behind a wife or husband, child or parent, brother or sister who were condemned to suffer. The survivors
hoped against hope for a miracle. Could their loved one be held in
a secret prison? Had their sons escaped execution and gone into
hiding? They were locked in agonizing limbo, unable to grieve, to
claim inheritance, to sell property, to remarry or – most poignantly
– to hold a funeral.

As one survivor put it, 'People are not needles. They cannot vanish for ever.' But the murderers had hidden their victims in ceme-
teries beneath marked graves; in wells and in caves, under heaps

of garbage, rubble and even animal carcasses. Bodies had been burned, dumped into rivers or secreted in remote fields surrounded by landmines and booby traps. In an elaborate effort to conceal their crimes, the perpetrators had even used heavy machinery to disperse the dead to secondary mass graves, once satellites had spotted the initial burial sites. The International Commission on Missing Persons (ICMP) began to track down and reassemble the disarticulated remains of victims from – in some cases – as many as four different locations.

Of all persons who went missing in the Yugoslav wars, almost half have yet to be found. Today, for the first time in history DNA is being used to reunite the living with their dead, bringing the hope of closure for individuals and, potentially, reconciliation between communities. This book documents the efforts of the organizations and the professionals – forensic scientists, humanitarian workers, civil servants – who work to release the bereaved from the anguish of their uncertainty by locating new burial grounds, exhuming unidentified bodies and piecing together scattered skeletons. Above all, *Missing Lives* gives a voice to the silenced victims and pays tribute to the tragedy of so many families.

The history of the Yugoslav wars is emotional and complicated. Ask a question about the Kosovo conflict for example and soon the discussion turns to the Second World War or even a fourteenth-century battle. In essence the wars began as a result of suppressed nationalism and raw political ambition. Since 1945 communist Yugoslavia had been held together by Tito's one-man dictatorship. With his death in 1980, frustrated politicians began to exploit nationalism in their bid for power. Chauvinistic mythologies were spun that exaggerated the people's differences. Wealthy Slovenia – no longer willing to bankroll the poorer republics – seceded from the federation in 1991. Croatia quickly followed only to be attacked by the Belgrade-controlled federal army under the pretext of protecting the Serbian minority in Croatia and defending Yugoslav unity. The conflict engulfed Bosnia and Herzegovina when that country declared its independence and the leading Bosnian Serb party opposed it. The war then escalated as the Serbian and Croatian presidents tried to divide Bosnia and Herzegovina between themselves. The later conflict in Kosovo, a region which Serbs consider to be the cradle of their culture, was a struggle of independence. The Bosnian and Kosovo conflicts could be ended only by extensive NATO bombing.

Suffering knows no borders. Young or old, male or female, Albanian, Bosniak, Croat and Serb, all face the same abyss. In the western Balkans most people – especially the families of the missing – speak now of the need to heal wounds. They plead for leaders to set an example and apologise for past wrongs. Some progress has been achieved. War criminals have been prosecuted and put behind bars in Belgrade, Sarajevo, Zagreb and Pristina. Former enemies work together to shed light on the fate of the thousands of persons still missing. But too few politicians in the region have shown the courage to act with contrition, to ask forgiveness for the sins inflicted by their predecessors.

The fifteen accounts in *Missing Lives* are haunting. The courage and dignity of the bereaved – who have lost much of their own lives as well as their loved ones – is humbling, inspiring and extraordinary. Theirs are stories which simply must be told.

Rory MacLean

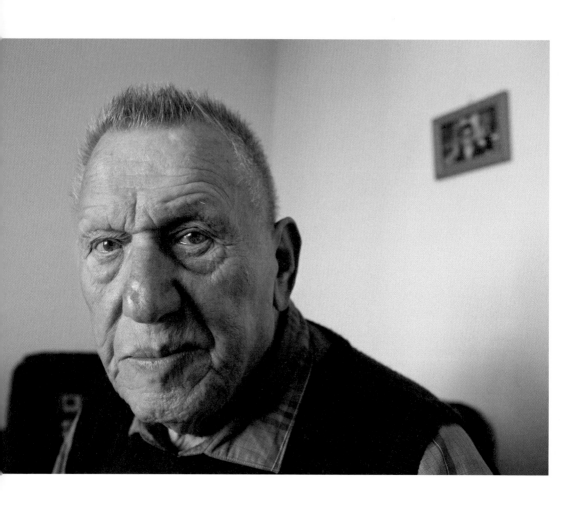

[Dragica and Drazen Tuskan]

Dawn broke over Vukovar, the soft rays of the rising sun brushing
the tops of the trees growing in and around the shell of the old
communist party club. Rosy shadows fell across the pulverised
brickwork of the Café Diksi. The facades of bullet-scarred apartment
blocks were pockmarked as if by a fatal rash.

'You need to understand that in the Balkans history is controlled
by politicians,' said Dragutin Tuskan, his watery blue eyes scanning
the city destroyed alongside the hope of a peaceful transition to
democracy. 'Here they create history.'

Tuskan is a haunted survivor. He was born 81 years ago near
Karlovac in the west of Croatia. During the Second World War the
Partisans – communist guerrillas who would later form the Yugoslav government – stole the blanket from his bed as well as his older
brother. The following year the Ustashi – Croat forces allied with
the Nazis – swept him away to war too.

'I was only 15 years old but no one could defy them,' he said,
turning the gold wedding band on his finger. 'We simply had to
fight.'

In the final days of the war Tuskan surrendered to the British
along with an estimated 50,000 defeated soldiers and 30,000
civilians at Bleiburg on the Austrian-Yugoslav border. The Ustashi
hoped to escape the victorious Partisans but they were abandoned
to their vengeful enemy.

'The Partisans were hiding in the forest,' recalled Tuskan. 'They
moved around us with knives, picking out individuals, asking "Do
you want to look at the sun?" When you lifted your head, they slit
your throat. The next day they stood us in lines and opened fire with

automatic weapons. I lay in pools of blood. I didn't know if I was dead or alive.'

The survivors were formed into four columns and marched over four months from the far north to the far south of the country. Tens of thousands died along the route. They ate only when sympathizers threw food into their ranks. Tuskan once caught and swallowed an egg, shell and all. His weight dropped to 34 kilos and – while repairing a road tunnel in Macedonia – he caught typhoid.

The massacre of prisoners of war at Bleiburg was the largest of its kind in the Second World War. The Slovenian Commission on Concealed Mass Graves has identified 570 related sites, from Bleiburg itself and the subsequent 'Mars Smrti' or Death March. In Croatia there are at least 190 mass graves, of which only one has been partially excavated. An estimated 16–18,000 bodies lie in the Tezno grave alone.

'So many fell along the roadside,' admitted Tuskan. 'Some bodies were even buried under the roads themselves.'

After the horror of war Tuskan longed for a quiet life. He moved as far away as possible from home without leaving Croatia. In pretty Vukovar on the Danube he married Dragica, found work as a salesman and bought a simple house on Kaciceva Street. Together they raised two sons.

Then in August 1991 Tuskan visited his elder son and pregnant English daughter-in-law in Zagreb. He'd planned to spend only the weekend away but the Yugoslav People's Army – successor of the Partisans – laid siege to Vukovar, cutting it off from the rest of Croatia.

'My wife and younger son were trapped. I was full of emotions. I couldn't go home,' he said.

When Croatia had declared independence from Yugoslavia,

Serbs living in Vukovar responded with armed insurrection. The
politics of ethnic intolerance had convinced them that their future
lay with Serbia across the Danube rather than in an independent
Croatia. The Yugoslav army and paramilitary groups supported the
insurrection, shelling the city with heavy artillery from August to
November, killing hundreds of people and reducing every neighbourhood to rubble. Tuskan's wife Dragica was hanging out the
washing when the armoured ground assault began. A grenade
landed in a nearby playground, its shrapnel hitting her arm and
stomach. She and their younger son Drazen made their way to the
hospital, which was considered to be the safest refuge in the city.
At the entrance door Drazen was shot in the leg.

The next day Vukovar fell. In Zagreb the ICRC secured an agreement between the Yugoslav army and Croatian authorities to place
the hospital, along with its war wounded and staff, under the protection of the Red Cross. But Yugoslav officers in Vukovar claimed
they were unaware of the agreement. They prevented the ICRC from
entering the hospital. They separated men from women. According
to an eye-witness, Dragica would not leave Drazen, clinging to his
leg as she was beaten to the ground. Around 250 wounded fighters
and civilians as well as hospital staff were loaded onto buses and
trucks. A crowd of local Serbs were reported to have shouted abuse
at the 'Ustashi murderers' as they were carried out on stretchers.
The prisoners were driven first to a military barracks, where an
unknown number of hospital staff were released, and then to a
nearby pig farm at Ovcara. The next day, the captives were executed
in cold blood by paramilitaries, their bodies dumped in a single
mass grave.

Of the 200 bodies later recovered, 190 have been identified.
Two senior Yugoslav army officers were found guilty of aiding and

abetting the torture and murder of the hospital prisoners by the International Criminal Tribunal for the former Yugoslavia.

Tuskan returned to Vukovar as soon as possible after the war. His house was a ruin without windows, doors or a roof. His bullet-riddled car – which Drazen had used both to reach the front line and to ferry the wounded to hospital – had been stolen. His beloved city was almost unrecognisable. Worst of all, neither Dragica or Drazen's remains could be found.

'For 17 years I haven't known where they are. During the day, during the night, I think about finding them, burying them, lighting candles for them,' Tuskan said, hitting his chest with his fist again and again. 'For these 17 years I didn't sing, didn't dance, nothing.'

When politicians control history, truth can be distorted for personal gain. Events are transformed into myths, facts lose their value and neighbours can be turned against each other. 'Yet no one has apologised,' Tuskan whispered. 'No one.'

These days with his eyesight failing he rarely leaves his elder son's house in Zagreb. When he does come back to Vukovar he visits the city's new cemetery. Beyond the haunting ranks of white crosses – where his wife and son should lie but do not – wait dozens of empty concrete frames. In these family members of Vukovar's defenders can be buried.

'I want to be buried here,' said Dragutin Tuskan. 'But I beg you to find their bodies for me before I die.'

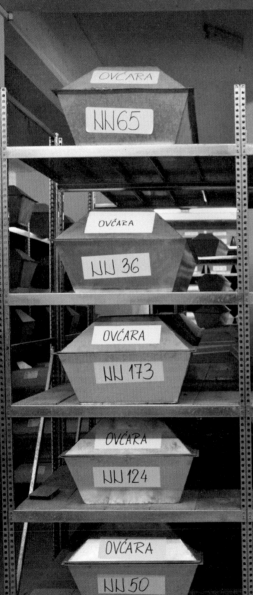
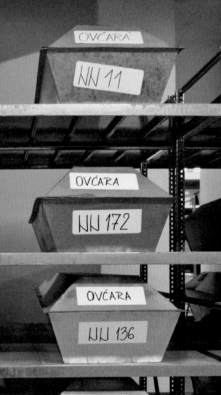
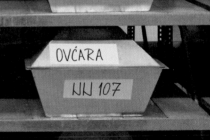
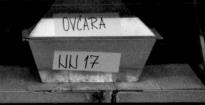

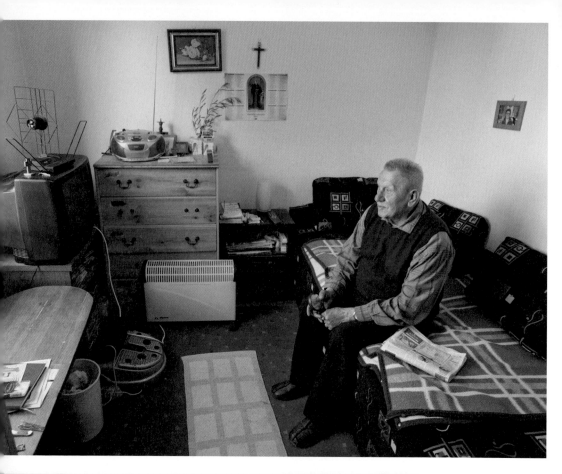

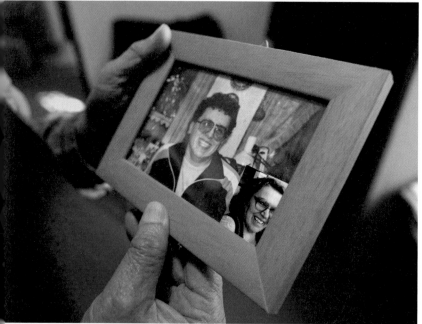

previous pages:
Unidentified bodies
from the Ovcara
massacre are stored
alongside 600 other
unknowns in the
Zagreb morgue.

above:
Tuskan in his make-
shift bedroom in
Zagreb. 'I don't want
to be a burden on
my elder son and his
family. But I came for
a weekend and have
stayed for 17 years.'

left:
Dragutin Tuskan's
wife and younger
son Drazen, 24, as
they looked shortly
before the war.

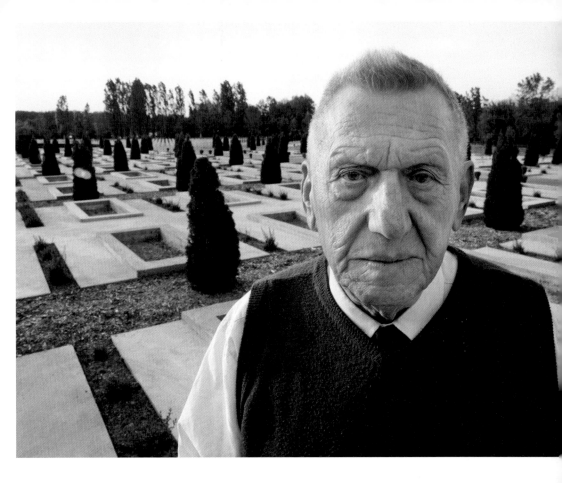

Tuskan wants to be
buried in Vukovar's
new cemetery in one
of the empty con-
crete frames reserved
for the families of
the city's defenders.

Tuskan at the Ovcara
memorial. The
bodies of his wife
Dragica and younger
son Drazen have
never been found.

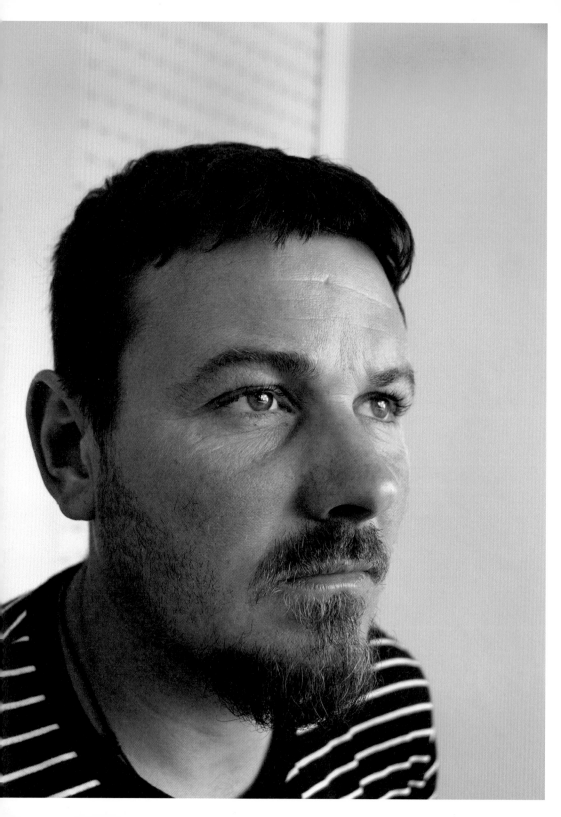

Zdenko Manjos
[Zvonko and Ivanka Manjos]

'It was an ordinary evening,' said Zdenko Manjos, looking down
at hands which seemed to belong to an older man. 'My sister and
I were at home with our parents in Vukovar. The electricity had
come on for the first time in months. Mama was putting on a wash.
Tata and a neighbour were fiddling with the television, twisting the
antenna this way and that. One moment we had a Serbian broad-
cast, the next it was Croatian. About 7.30pm the front bell rang.
A man stood at the door, asking politely for Tata. He said that he
was from State Security – he showed his card – and wanted Tata to
come to the police station to answer a few questions about what
he had done in the war. Tata left wearing his slippers. He had no
jacket or fear. I didn't pay much attention.'

Zdenko closed his broad, rough hands over his neat beard and
went on, 'About thirty minutes later a second man came to the door.
He asked Mama to come to the station and confirm Tata's statement.
She left her washing and walked out the door. She didn't take a coat
either.' He shrugged and stared at the floor. 'It was an ordinary evening. I wasn't expecting to never see my parents again.'

Zdenko's father was Ruthenian. His mother was a Serb. The children
grew up a stone's throw from the Danube. His father had a little
boat and – when work allowed – he and his son went fishing together, camping on the riverbank. At home Zdenko's father loved to
play the accordion and sing, his wife laughing at his side. Theirs was
a mixed marriage and so, rather than with a specific ethnic group,
they identified themselves with the river. The Danube – rather than
nationalism – could be said to run in their blood.

Early in 1992 the family had moved to Borovo Naselje on the outskirts of Vukovar. By then the city had been occupied by the Serbian forces and hostilities ceased. Like many teenagers, Zdenko had been assigned to work for the Civilian Protection Unit, clearing away the rubble and helping to replace windows in public buildings. His sister Natasa, who was 16 at the time, looked forward to starting high school.

Zdenko and Natasa waited all that night for their parents to return home. Early the next morning their hearts leapt on hearing a key in the lock, but it was only their grandmother.

Zdenko, who was 18 years old, went first to the local police station. A neighbour then drove him to the Vukovar barracks and to Erdut to talk to the new civilian government. No one in the war-torn region was willing or able to give him information on the where-abouts of his parents.

'We thought maybe Tata was in prison. We thought that Mama might telephone,' said Zdenko, calling them by the names he'd used for them in childhood, their relationship cut short and frozen in time. 'But at the same time we couldn't stop ourselves from imagining deeper possibilities.'

Over the next weeks Zdenko and Natasa wrote Red Cross letters – the ICRC has been delivering messages to prisoners since the First World War – even though they had no postal address for their parents. Natasa moved in with her grandmother, starting work rather than high school. Zdenko was drafted into the occupying army, later finding jobs on building sites and learning to drive a fork-lift truck. He couldn't touch the family's savings or sell the apartment because his parents – who had been declared missing rather than dead – had no official status.

'I am the child of a mixed marriage. My sister and I were raised

as Yugoslav children. After the war we no longer knew who we were. 23
I was not Croat. I wasn't Serb. So we didn't receive compensation
from either side.'

Fifteen years after their disappearance the bodies of Zdenko's parents were identified a hundred miles away in Serbia. His mother's
remains had been discovered in Novi Sad, his father's in Belgrade.
Two laboratories in two different cities had made the DNA match
in the same week. His mother's skull had been fractured. Too little
of his father remained to perform a conclusive autopsy. During the
wars in the former Yugoslavia, 426 unidentified bodies had floated
down the Danube and the Sava into Serbia. Zdenko's parents were
among them. In 1992 they had been buried in separate graves
marked 'Unknown'. In time and with the advances in technology,
the bodies were exhumed and bone samples taken to the ICMP for
analysis. The DNA matched that of Zdenko and Natasa's blood.

'In our old village there's a rumour about why my parents were
killed,' said Zdenko. 'A villager who happened to have the same
name as Tata – Zvonko Manjos – had joined the Croat forces, and
gone missing in action. Serb State Security may have been looking
for him, and picked up my father instead.'

Or perhaps Zvonko and Ivanka Manjos lost their lives simply because their names sounded foreign, which was a deadly liability in a
region where the importance of ethnicity had swelled to grotesque
proportions. On their death certificates the cause of death was
recorded simply as 'War'.

Today Zdenko appears both calm and wounded, at once welcoming and wary of strangers. He is married and has been blessed
with two children. His sister Natasa also has children of her own.

'My wife is a Serb with Croatian blood,' he said, shaking his head

as if to make sense of the absurdity of his parents' murder. 'My aunt is a Ruthenian married to a Croat. Every year we celebrate two Christmases; a Catholic one in Zagreb and then an Orthodox one here in Vukovar. Everything is mixed.'

When work and family life allow, Zdenko finds solace by going fishing.

'I love the Danube,' he said, looking out over the river. 'My father and I used to swim across it, to a sandy beach on the opposite, Serbian side. Not any more.'

Zdenko shook his head again and cast his line into the cold water.

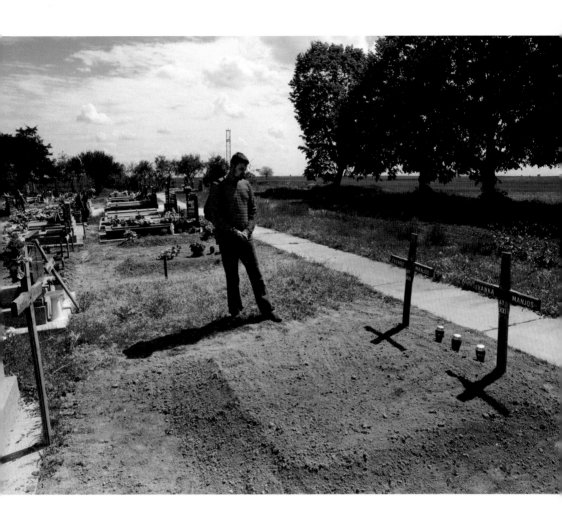

Fifteen years after their disappearance, Zdenko was finally able to bury his parents.

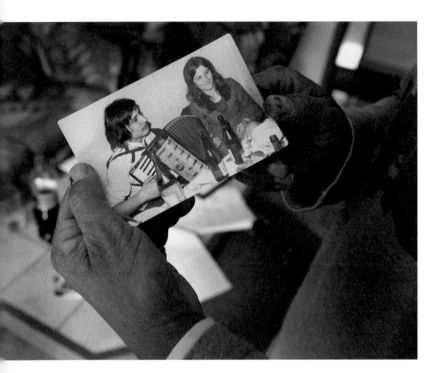

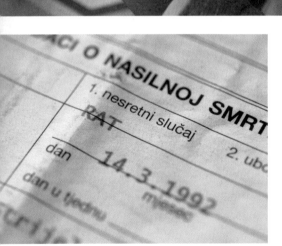

top:
Zdenko still doesn't
know why his par-
ents were murdered.
They were probably
killed by mistake.

above:
Cause of Death: WAR

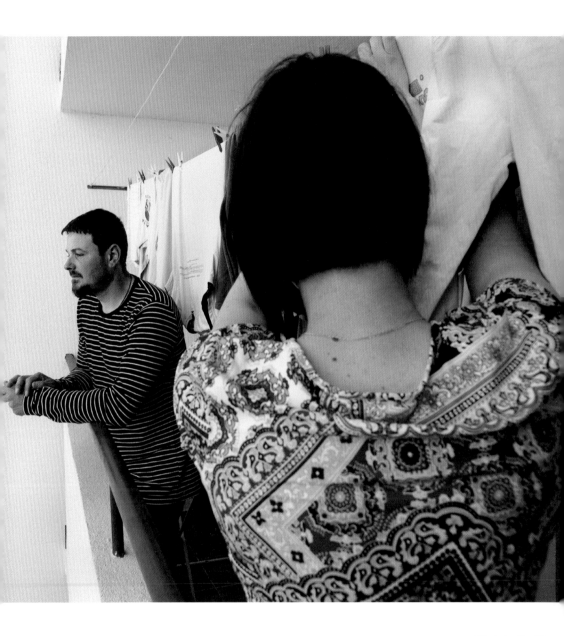

Zdenko's wife still fears for the family's safety. Seventeen years after the abduction of her parents-in-law, she is unwilling to allow her children to be photographed.

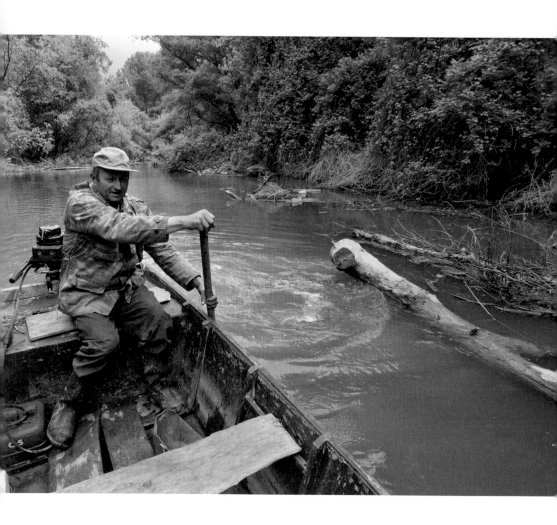

Three months after
their disappearance
in Vukovar, Ivanka
Manjos' body was
found by this fisher-
man 109 km down
river near Novi Sad.

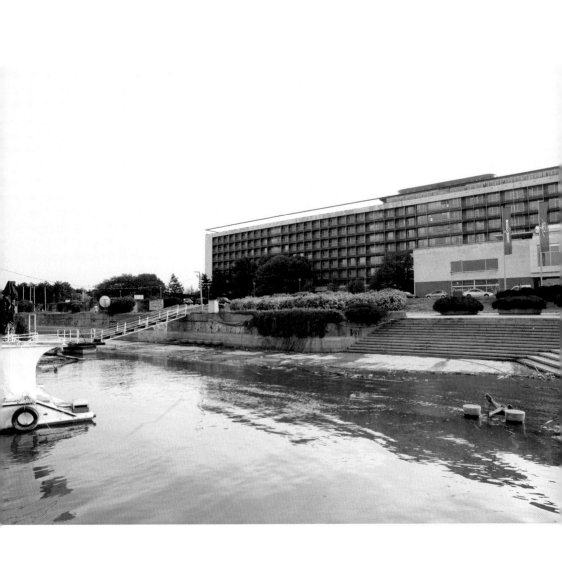

Zvonko Manjos' body
was washed ashore a
further 50 km down
the Danube in front
of the Hotel Yugosla-
via in New Belgrade.

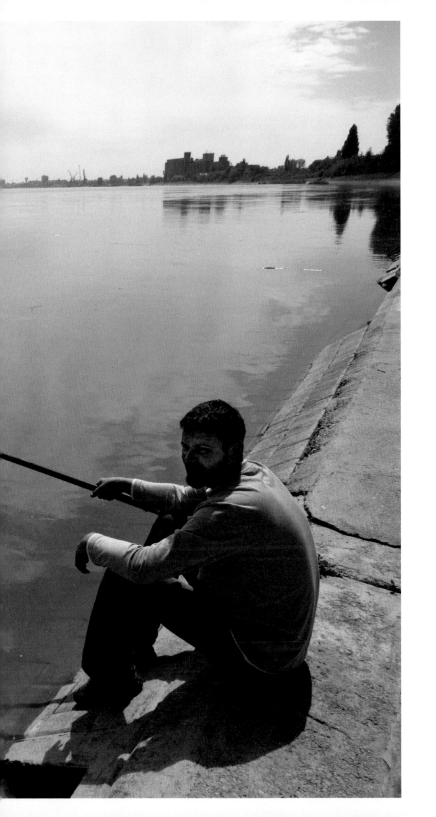

Like his parents,
Zdenko loves the
Danube and fishes
as often as work and
family life allow.

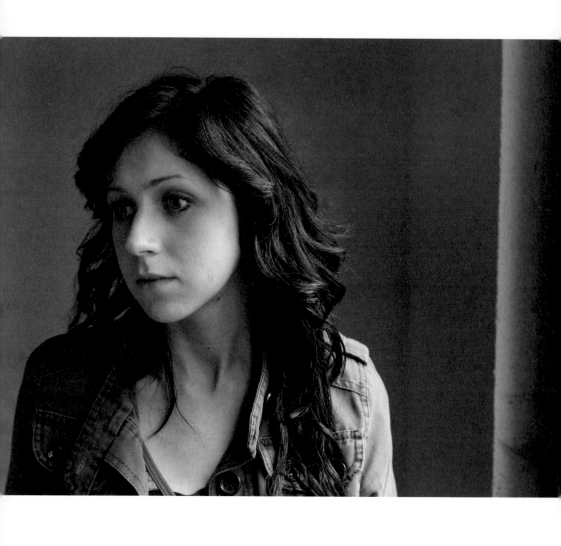

[Esad, Fatima, Adis and Adisa Salkic]

A dozen doves wheeled around a minaret, their bellies and wings flashing white in the clear spring sunshine. Beneath them slender, elegant gravestones marched towards eternity, or lost their earthly balance and tilted wildly at the ground. Beyond them, in a nest of shabby apartment blocks at the far end of Travnik, Alisa Salkic, 18, sat with her best friend Nisveta and said, 'I learnt the truth here on this sofa.'

The colour began to drain from her face.

'I had just washed my hair, and Secira was plaiting it, and I was cuddling her and telling her that she was the best mother in the world when, suddenly, she started to cry. "I want to tell you the truth," confessed Secira, the woman who for nine years Alisa had believed to be her mother. "You know the photograph of the stranger which you keep asking me about? She is your real mother."'

Alisa had been born not in Travnik but rather in Nadioci, a nearby hamlet on the outskirts of Ahmici in Bosnia. Her father Esad had owned a small grocery store in the village. He was a faithful Communist, devoted to Tito, convinced that all Yugoslavs were brothers. Her mother Fatima was the middle child of three sisters, the kindest one, the one who had always been ready to help her neighbours. Together Esad and Fatima had three children, Alisa being the youngest. She was only a toddler when the war started between Croats and Bosniaks. One day uniformed Croat Defence Council (HVO) soldiers came into their house, tied Esad to a chair and in front of the family beat him and then shot him, first through his feet, then in his

knees, next in the arms and shoulders, finally through the head. Afterwards a Croat neighbour told Fatima, 'You never expected us to be the ones to kill you. We are happy to surprise you.'

Fatima had rung her sister Secira in Travnik and begged her to come to Nadioci. The first two children were old enough to walk and so would be able to escape into the hills. But Alisa was too little so Secira offered to take her back to the city. Two weeks later, the HVO shelled Ahmici and the surrounding villages. Over 180 Bosniak houses and two mosques were destroyed. According to the European Union Monitoring Mission and other observers, Bosniaks were burnt alive, a three-month-old baby was machine-gunned in his crib and fleeing civilians were herded into a field where elite marksmen waited to shoot them. Twenty-three members of the Salkic family vanished. Fatima, together with her two children and twenty other families, were last seen riding away from the village on a tractor.

In the Travnik apartment Alisa leaned her head on Nisveta's shoulder. Her khaki, kohled eyes had about them a look of wonder – or shock. In a strong yet strained voice she said, 'Nisveta was the first person who I told.'

'Was I?'

Alisa nodded.

'I remember you telling me after school that you once had a brother and sister, showing me the photographs.'

'I look completely like my father,' Alisa volunteered. 'The same nose, eyebrows – I recognise him in me.' She paused then added, 'At first the news that I'd lost my parents wasn't a big deal. I was so young. It didn't feel tragic. But now whenever there's a programme

about the war on television, or I hear my aunt and uncle talking
about it, I have to leave the room. I feel something so huge is
missing.'

Every other month Alisa's uncle Hasan Tarakcija drives her to her
old village. As the only surviving Salkic, Alisa inherited the house
and land. She hopes to sell it to pay her university fees and to buy
herself an apartment. Both girls have begun training to be nurses.
Nisveta wants to practice in Travnik. Alisa plans to move away to
Sarajevo.

Nadioci lies off the main road in a steep, leafy valley of arrest-
ing beauty. When they arrived the nearest neighbour came out to
meet Alisa and her uncle. His gestures were forced, his laughter
too loud. Alisa would not shake his hand. Later inside the empty,
partly-restored family house she said, 'It's unbelievable how people
pretend, even today. They act like friends, offer food and drinks.
I simply can't grasp how it's possible.' Her nostrils flared. 'They
killed my parents.'

'He's just frightened,' said Hasan, nodding out of the window
at the neighbour. 'He and his wife hid inside when the soldiers were
here.'

Almost ten years have passed since Alisa gave a blood sample
to the ICMP but no DNA match has yet been found. The remains
of her mother, her brother and sister, her paternal uncles and
their children, grandparents and other relatives remain missing.
Only the resting place of her father is known.

Hasan walked up through the village, past the burnt out shells
of Salkic houses and the well-kept homes of Croat villagers. A
child's pink scooter lay in a driveway. A boy brought sheep down
from the hills. At the top of the valley of plum and apple orchards,

in an overgrown glade, stood eight slender gravestones, some standing straight, others tilting at the ground. Among them was a low mound of earth, the unmarked grave of Alisa's father. In the two weeks before she herself was murdered, Alisa's mother hadn't been able to have a stone carved. Birds sang in the trees. Sheep bells rang in the distance. Hasan said a quiet prayer. Alisa has never been to this place.

Back at the house, she said, 'I never allow myself to imagine how life would have been if the war hadn't happened.'

She and her friend Nisveta were anxious to leave the village and return to Travnik. 'Neither of us like history at school,' volunteered Nisveta. 'We prefer going out with friends, lots of friends, and drinking coffee. In any case, the history we're taught stops with Tito. The war isn't spoken about at school.'

As they stepped back into her uncle's Golf, Alisa added stoically, 'Would it be better not to have known the truth? No, even though it has brought pain. As time passes by, my story would have been forgotten. I want it to be told.'

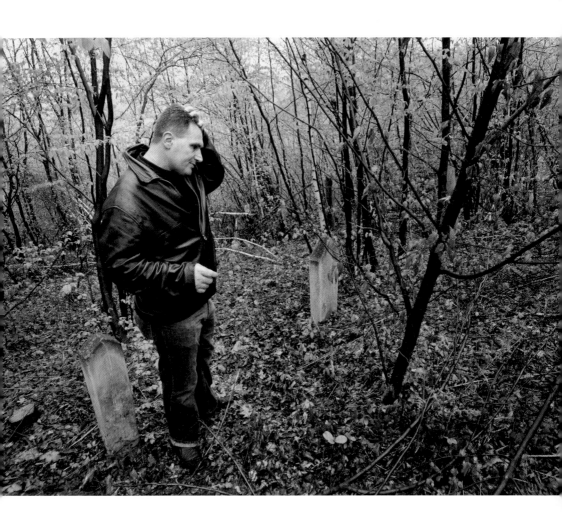

Alisa's uncle Hasan
Tarakcija stands in
the overgrown Salkic
family cemetery.
At his feet is the
unmarked grave of
Alisa's father. Alisa
has never seen it.

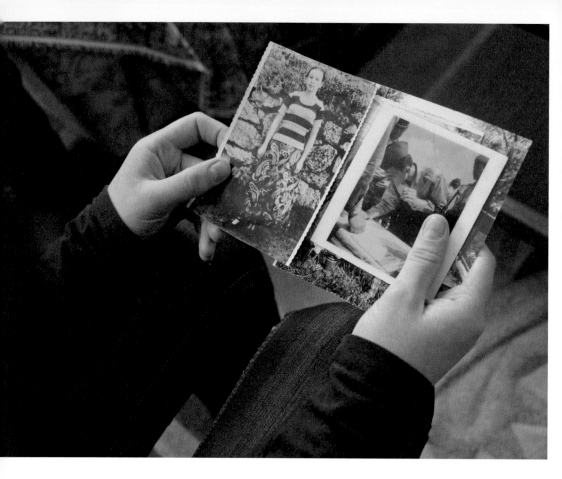

Alisa's parents Esad
and Fatima were
killed along with
22 relatives during
Croatian attacks
on Ahmici and sur-
rounding villages.

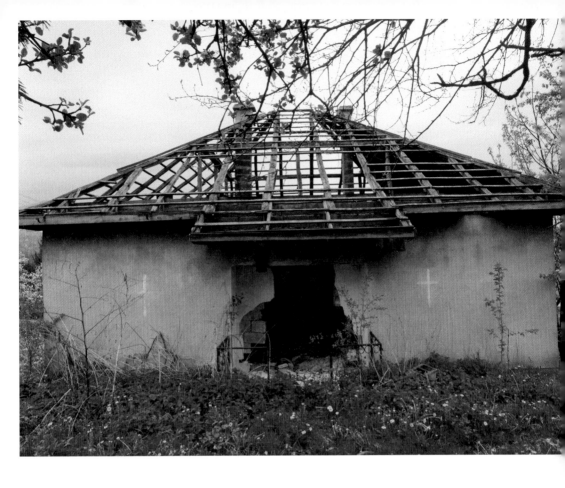

Before burning
Bosniak houses,
soldiers of the HVO –
the Croatian Defence
Council – often
painted Christian
crosses on the walls.

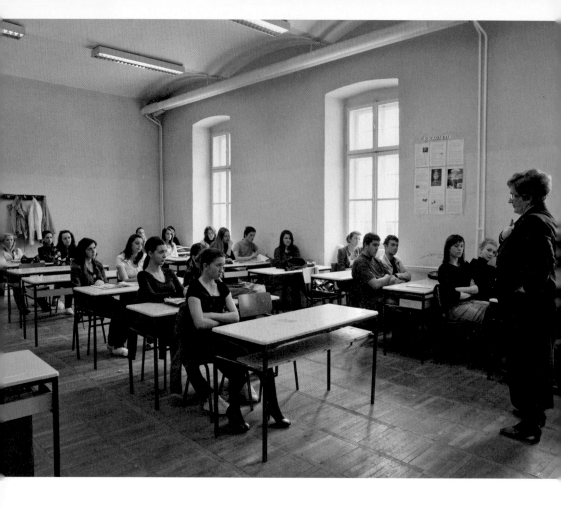

Alisa and her best friend Nisveta maintain that nationality isn't an issue for them. There are Croats in their class at school, many of whom are Nisveta's friends. But all Alisa's friends are Bosniaks.

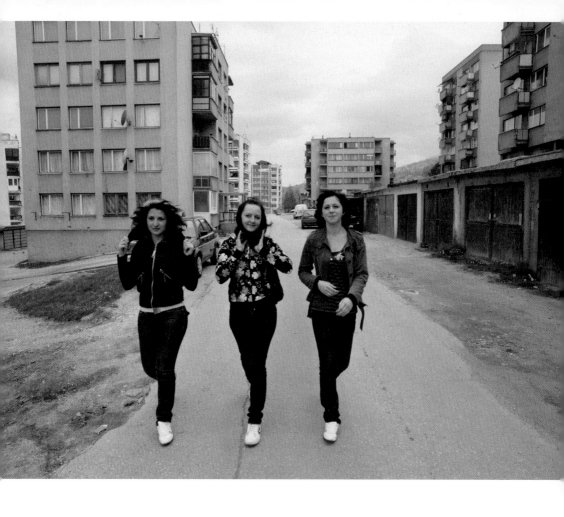

In Travnik Alisa
Salkic, right, walks
to school with her
cousin and Nisveta.
The girls have been
best friends since
Grade 1.

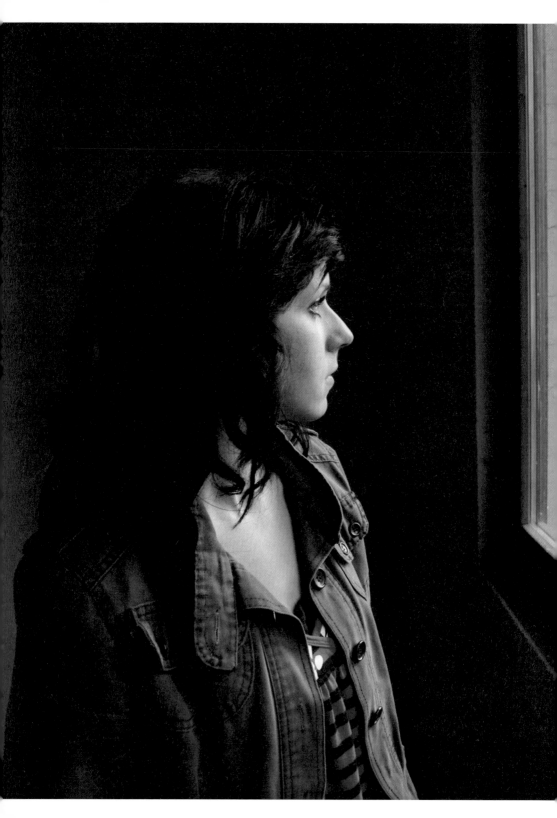

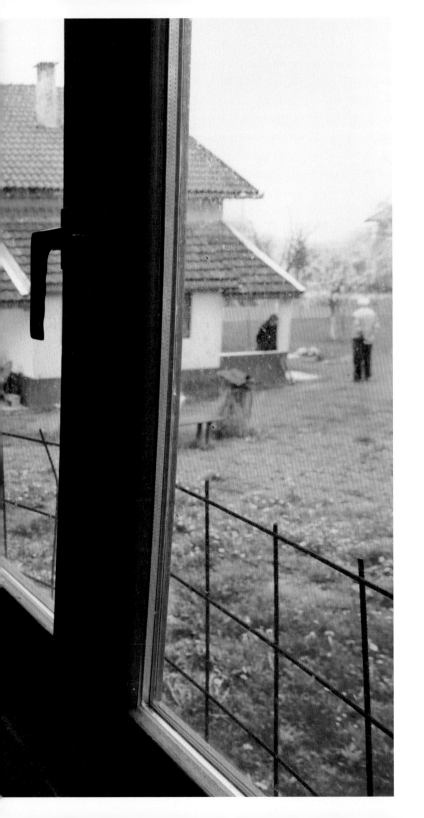

Alisa looks out from the room where her father was executed. 'It's unbelievable how people pretend, even today. They act like friends, offer food and drinks. I simply can't grasp how it's possible,' she said.

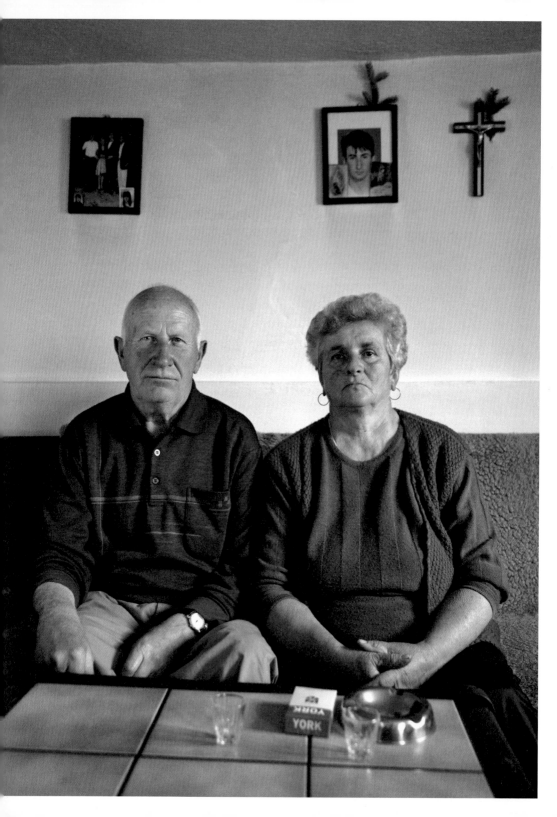

[Ivica Budimirovic]

'What eyes can see, his hands could make', said Milka Budimirovic.
'That was our son Ivica. He loved making things with wood, with
metal, with electrics...'

'He bought a little Fiat 500...' interrupted her husband Anto.

'An *orange* Fiat,' Milka carried on. 'He loved bright colours and
people too.'

'He wired up a small television set in the car, parked right in
front of the house and crammed his friends into the car, and all
around it, to watch a big football match.'

'It was a Dinamo Zagreb game.'

'Ivica was crazy about football.'

'He supported Dinamo Zagreb. I preferred Celik, the local Bosnian team,' said Anto.

Their two-storey, terracotta-tiled house sat high above the Bos-
na river, on the western side of the valley, surrounded by blossom-
ing fruit trees. Beyond the low doorway and hallway kitchen was a
low-ceilinged living room. On its wall hung a crucifix, a photograph
of their son and a single struggling creeper starved of light.

'He was 18 when he was drafted into the then-Yugoslav Army,'
said Milka, her fingers pulling at her weave of tightly curled grey
hair. 'After his first month's service, we were invited to visit the
camp. When we arrived the soldiers crowded around us saying,
"Ivica cuts our hair. Ivica painted the barrack door." We met his Commanding Officer who told us, "You should be proud to have a son
like this. I am proud to have him as a soldier."'

'He was a border guard,' hurried Anto, as impatient as his wife to
share their son's story. 'He liked the work because he patrolled with

a dog. He loved animals.'

'He was away from home for 15 months,' continued Milka. 'It was meant to be exactly one year but, at the last minute, he was ordered to stay for an extra three months. If they hadn't done that everything would be different today.'

In the late spring of 1992 Ivica and a few fellow soldiers at the end of their national service had been flown by helicopter to Banja Luka, some 200 kilometres from his home in Zenica. The war was just beginning in Bosnia and the multi-ethnic Yugoslav army was transforming itself into a Serbian force. Ivica called his parents to ask if there was shooting in Doboj, the halfway point between the two cities.

'We didn't know that there was trouble,' recalled Milka, a haunted echo in her voice. 'We told him to come home on the bus. He was less than three hours' ride away.'

That afternoon Milka had made up his bed, cleaned his room, began cooking his favourite burek beef pie. Anto had told the neighbours and called the family's friends. All night the garden had been full of people, but Ivica never arrived.

'Around midnight a taxi drove up our street. We were sure it was him. But it wasn't.' As Milka's spirit and heart sank a chill seemed to descend on the room. She heaved herself up from the sofa to feed cut logs into the stove, sparks flying toward her weathered face. 'He was a good boy. He didn't drink or smoke, like I do now.' She sat back down heavily on the sofa. 'He simply didn't come home.'

The next morning Milka had called his Commanding Officer who told her only what she knew, that Ivica had reached Banja Luka. She made enquiries at municipal and state offices, registered his disappearance with the Red Cross, pleaded with Zenica's mayor to go to Banja Luka. But come the summer, fighting had closed the

roads and cut telephone lines. No one could help them in their
search.

'I hoped that he would find a way to us,' said Anto, speaking quietly now. 'We knew the stories of people going missing for 20 or 30 years and then being found alive.'

'I lived in hope too,' said Milka. 'But in the hope of just finding him, dead or alive. Knowing nothing was the worst for me. I'm a religious person. I needed to end the agony.'

In parts of Bosnia, the ethnic patchwork was reminiscent of a leopard's skin; patches of Croats, surrounded by Bosniaks, rubbing up against areas of Serbs. During the war the patchwork moved, as if the leopard were running, or springing in attack. Ivica had simply been unlucky, passing across the skin of the leopard and along a road which happened to become one of the war's front lines.

In 1992 his body had been dumped in a ditch and buried without ceremony alongside two slain Bosniaks in the Doboj town cemetery. His name was recorded in the register but no one had bothered to find and inform the family. No one took responsibility for his murder. No one considered the pointlessness of killing a young man on the way home at the end of his military service.

Nine long years later Ivica's remains were found then identified by the ICMP. In his pocket was a bus ticket to Zenica, as well as his comb, a health booklet and half-burnt Yugoslav banknotes.

'No one knows why he was killed,' said Anto, looking down at the table, aligning the tablecloth. 'We don't know who did it.' He hesitated. 'It seems that he was beaten to death with a metal bar.'

The ICRC had accompanied the Budimirovics through the identification process. Milka wailed when she first saw the familiar possessions, then she became calm.

'We are Catholics,' she had said. 'Our custom is to dress the de-

ceased in new clothes. Please would you leave me to dress my son.'

All that morning she had carried a small holdall with her. She opened it then, as well as the coffin. Her son's remains had been placed in a white plastic body bag. With infinite care she pulled a new shirt and a new pair of trousers over the white bag. She didn't cry. When she had finished she said, 'I have done my best. He was my only son.'

In their front room, Milka looked up from her raw, empty hands and recalled, 'A part of my agony vanished that day. For so many years I had worried where he was, if he was hungry, if he was cold. At last I know where he is.' She gasped to catch her breath. 'But I can't sleep at night any more.'

Ivica was reburied in the Perinhan cemetery just down the road from their home. His grave overlooks the same valley, the same river, the same fruit trees that he knew as a boy. Every day Milka and Anto walk through the dandelions and long grass to his grave.

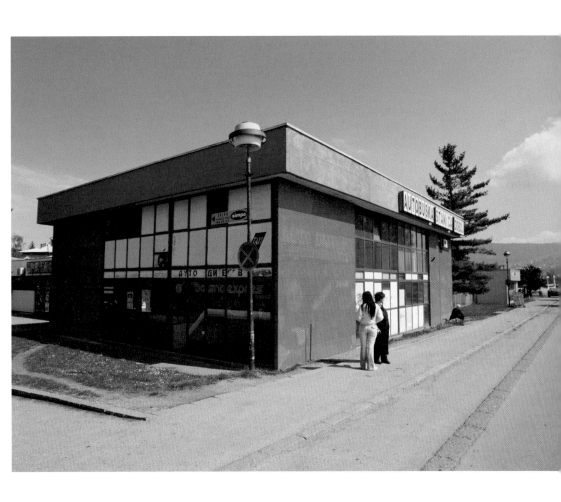

Ivica Budimirovic
went missing when
returning home
from military service.
It was at the Doboj
coach station that he
was allegedly taken
off a bus.

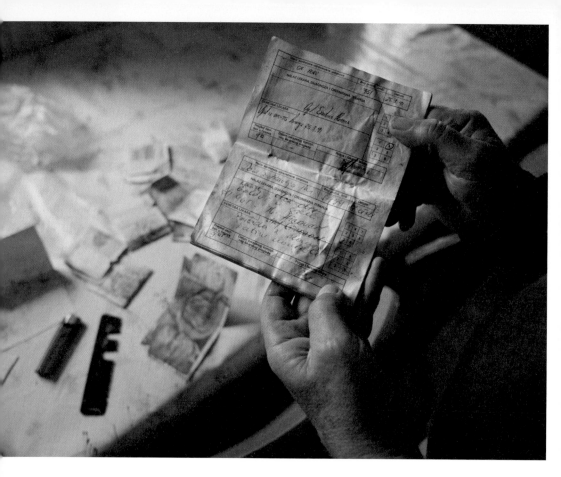

Ivica was beaten to
death with an iron
bar and bundled
fully-clothed into
an unmarked grave.
His parents have
kept the bus ticket
to Zenica, his comb,
a health booklet
and the half-burnt
Yugoslav banknotes
that were found later
in his pocket.

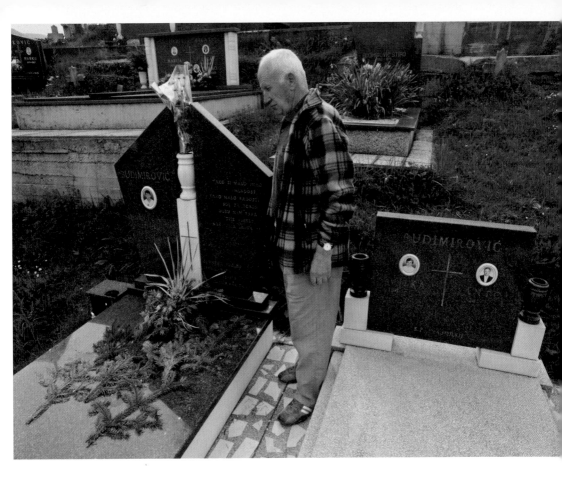

Nine years after
his disappearance,
Ivica's remains were
found, disinterred
and reburied in a
cemetery near to his
home. Milka and
Anto built his new
tomb with their own
hands, next to their
own, wishing never
to be separated from
their son again.

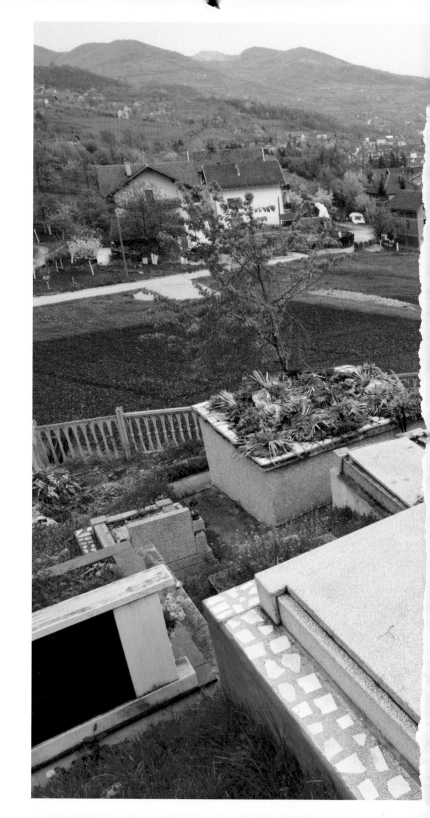

'At last I know where
he is,' said Milka.
'But I can't sleep at
night any more.'

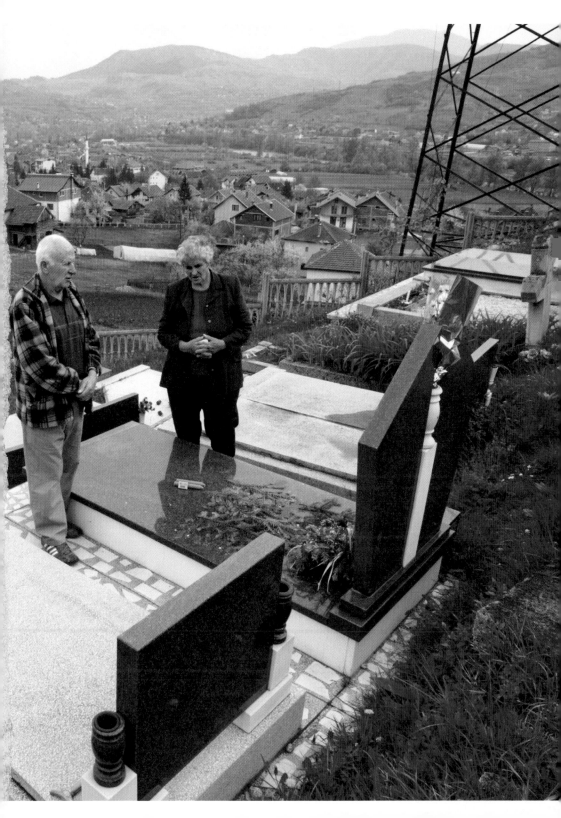

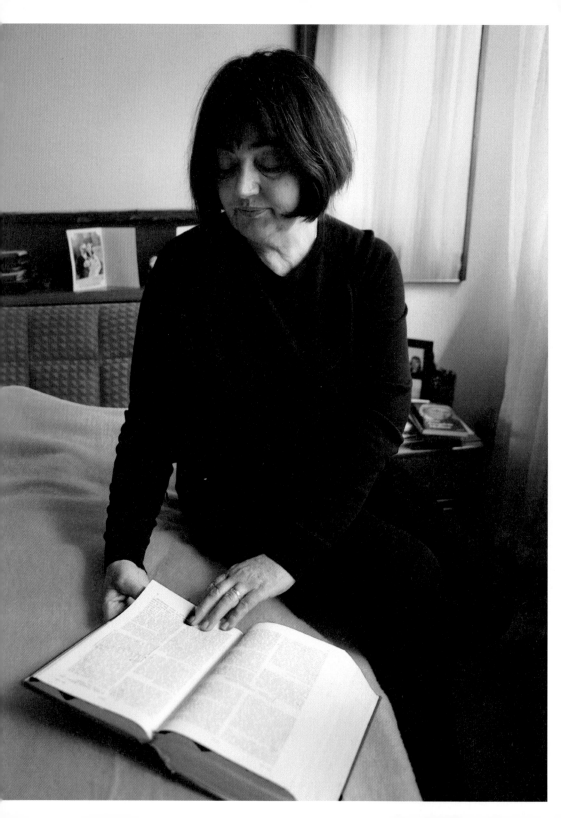

Tonka Pezelj
[Judge Miljenko Pezelj]

'My Miljenko was an intellectual *par excellence,*' said Tonka Pezelj, opening her shoebox of mementoes, spreading his legal articles and poetry across the dining table. 'The courthouse was his second home.'

When a city or region is seized by force, and its old administration removed, compliant professionals are needed to smooth the transition to the new authority. In September 1991 when Serbs established their self-styled breakaway republic in Croatia, Miljenko Pezelj was president of the Petrinja district court. The incomers wanted him as a collaborator.

A few weeks earlier his wife Tonka – a high school teacher – had returned home from a holiday on the Adriatic with their children. Miljenko, who'd spent the summer at court, was busy covering the building's windows with sheets of plywood to protect them from an anticipated Serbian attack. Tonka pleaded with her husband to move with her to safety in Zagreb, the Croatian capital. He told her that his duty was to stay in Petrinja.

'I remember going through our house for the last time touching our books,' she said. 'We had such a library: Proust, Joyce, Kafka, Tolstoy, Andric. But I felt I could only take one book with me, so I chose the Bible. Miljenko used to read it every night before bed, filling the margins with notations. It was our book, and it had always been beside our bed.'

Tonka drove to Zagreb to be with the children. A few days later Petrinja was occupied and cut off from Croatia. Suddenly there was no telephone contact. No open roads. No word.

56

'It's hard to count the number of doors I knocked on to get news of him,' said Tonka. 'Twice a week I visited the International Red Cross in Zagreb. I met with the European monitoring mission. I even contacted the Yugoslav army.' The military told her to forget her husband as he was probably not interested in her any longer. When UN soldiers arrived to monitor secessionist Krajina, as the breakaway region called itself, Tonka asked a friend to translate a few words into English. She wrote them on a card to show to the peacekeepers, their phonetic rendition on the reverse for her to read aloud. 'My husband Miljenko Pezelj stayed in Petrinja and I want to know if he is alive. He was born on the 20th of February 1939. His address in Petrinja is Kajetana Knezica Street, number 7. He is a judge.'

Miljenko had been placed under house arrest by the new Serbian authorities. During eight months of captivity, only four letters were smuggled out of Petrinja to Tonka and their children. Miljenko addressed them as 'my dear refugees'. In them he reported on his life alone in their home. There was neither electricity nor neighbours on the street. He baked bread in a wood-fired oven until the flour ran out. He read by candlelight, rationing himself to a quarter of candle every night. Every morning he thanked God for allowing him to live to see another day. He said that Sisak – the neighbouring town across the front line where Tonka worked – felt as far away as Siberia.

Most movingly, Miljenko used the fabric of the house as a blank page. With a felt-tip pen he recorded hundreds of thoughts and events on the kitchen walls and tiles. On 6 December he noted the first snowfall of winter. On 8 December he wished his mother a happy birthday. On 5 April he reported the burning of a neighbour's

house. He wrote down overheard sentences whispered between his
captors '...the evidence is that he'll be prosecuted but he has to feel
we're on his side...' On the kitchen doorframe he quoted the words
of Ivo Andric, the Bosnian-born Nobel prize laureate, 'Our human-
ity is defined by our behaviour toward our fellow man.'

Then at 11pm on 11 May Miljenko wrote, 'Police ordered me to
open the door. I refused.' Eight days later they broke it down and
killed him.

That same evening in Zagreb, Tonka suddenly awoke and cried,
'Miljenko!' The next day at school she couldn't concentrate, staring
instead out of the window towards Petrinja. She knew in her heart
that something terrible had happened to her husband.

Three years later Croat forces retook the area and Croat residents
were finally allowed to return to the town. Tonka walked towards
their old house, hardly recognising the route.

'I felt as if my feet weren't touching the ground,' she said. 'I felt
as if the dead of Petrinja – all the 300 lost civilians – were walking
beside me. Somehow I found our house. The upper floor was gone.
I walked from one room to another feeling senseless. For four years
I had dreamt of coming home, now it was like the sky was falling
on me.'

The house was a wreck. All their books were gone. Squatters
had grubbed up their roses and wisteria and replaced them with
potatoes. Among the ashes she found her wedding photographs.

Tonka went on, 'Then I went into the kitchen and discovered the
tiles. I wept when I saw his handwriting.'

In time she learnt that Miljenko had been given a final ultima-
tum to cooperate with the new Serbian court. His refusal had cost
him his life. The crime scene report, found in archives abandoned

by the fleeing authorities, recorded that Judge Miljenko Pezelj had been killed at home, dying of gunshot wounds in his garden. The report included a precise drawing of the house, garden and location of the body.

Miljenko had been buried in the overgrown Orthodox part of the town cemetery. As soon as possible Tonka had his body exhumed and reburied in the family plot in the Catholic section.

'When I reburied him, I was suddenly calm. For the first time in years my heart beat normally. At last he was resting where he had to rest, and I could visit him at the cemetery and talk... talk... talk about all those things which had been left unspoken.'

'There is no greater suffering than not knowing where a loved one is buried,' declared Tonka. 'Yet there are many people alive today who know the location of gravesites and say nothing. They cannot conceive of the extent of pain caused by their silence.'

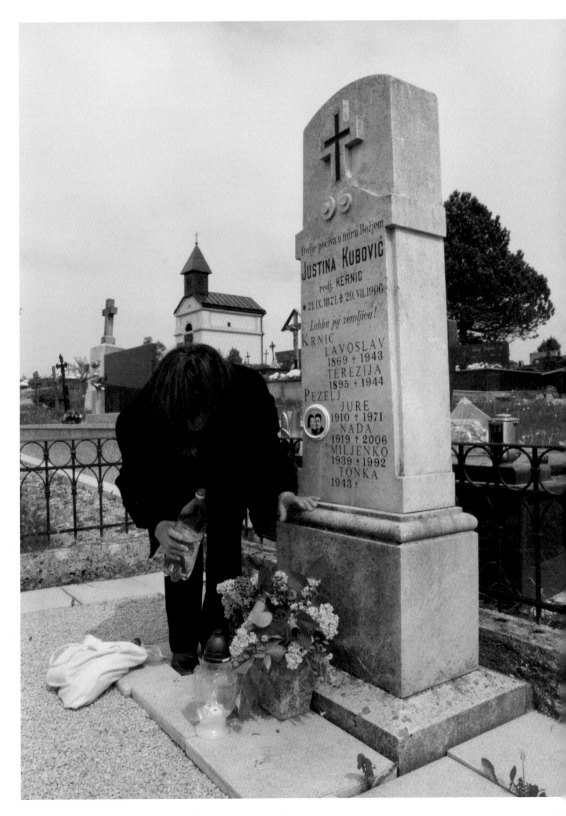

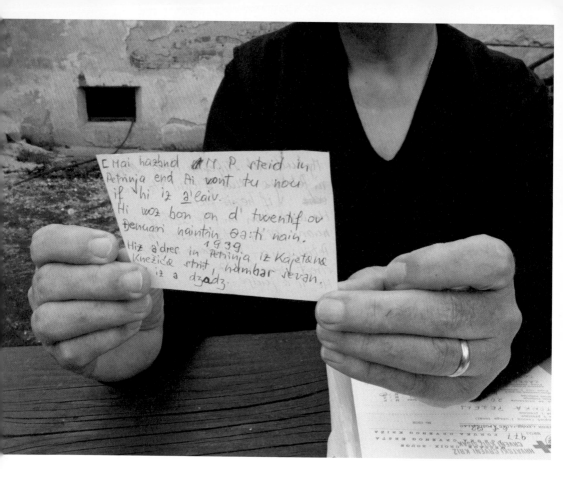

previous page:
After his murder
Miljenko, a Catholic,
was buried in the
Orthodox section of
Petrinja cemetery.
Tonka had his body
exhumed and rebur-
ied in the family plot.

above:
Tonka holds the
phonetic rendition
of the plea she read
out to UN peacekeep-
ers. 'My husband
Miljenko Pezelj
stayed in Petrinja and
I want to know if he
is alive...'

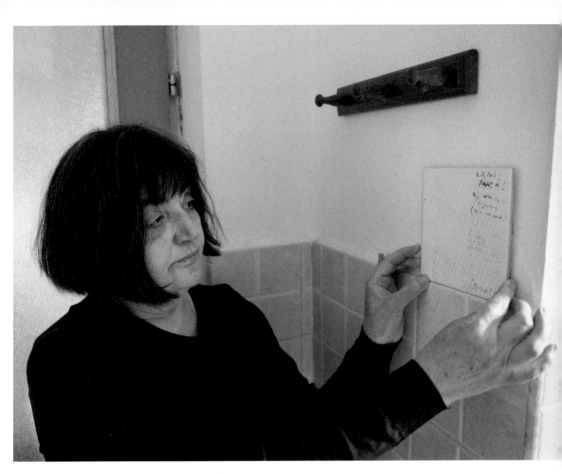

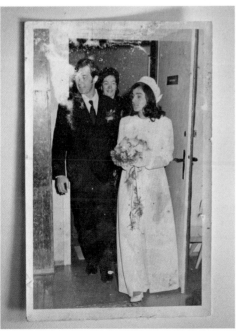

above:
During his eight
months under house
arrest Judge Miljenko
Pezelj used the
fabric of the house
as a diary, record-
ing hundreds of
thoughts and events
on the kitchen tiles
and walls.

left:
Four years after her
husband's arrest,
Tonka was finally
allowed to return to
Petrinja. Among the
ashes of her home
she found her wed-
ding photograph.

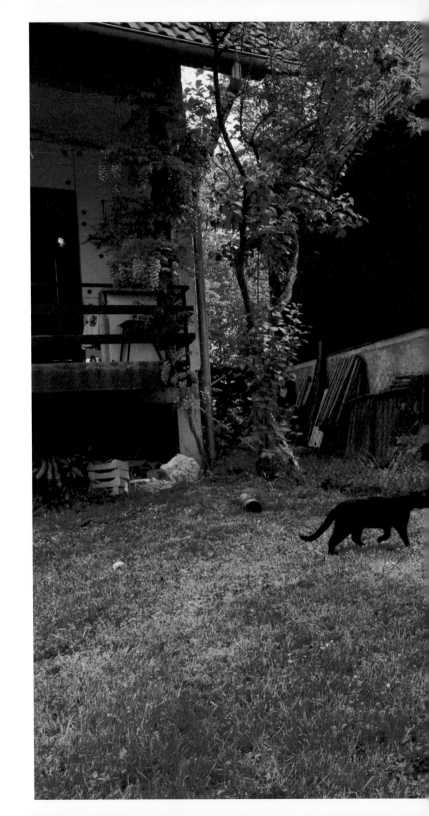

Tonka with her
cats in the garden
where her husband
Miljenko died of
gunshot wounds.
Every night she lights
a lamp at the spot.

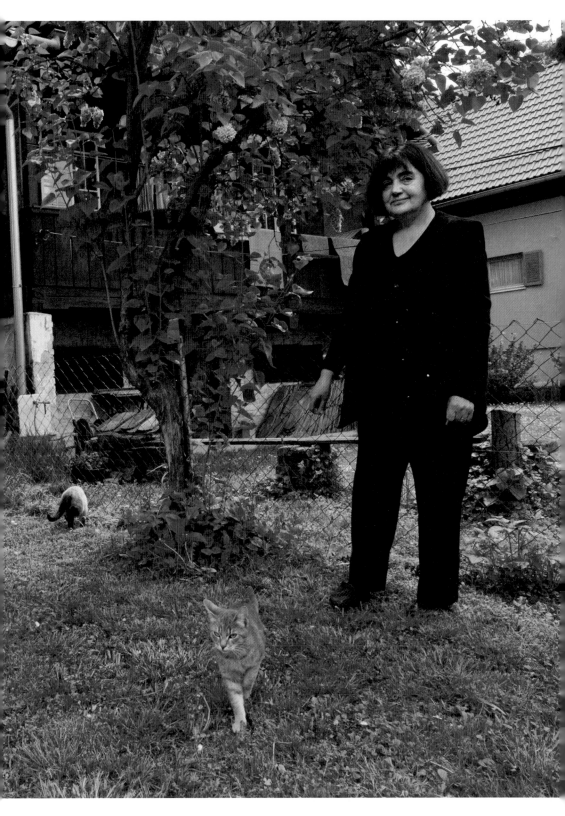

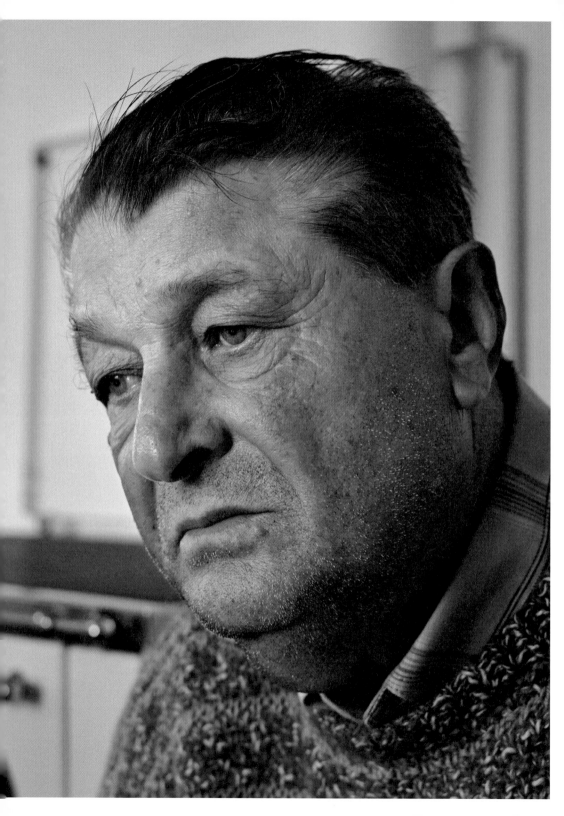

[Edin and Emir Elezovic]

'All this land once belonged to our family,' said Muharem Elezovic, sweeping his arm across the bare fields. 'They took it – and our sons – away from us.'

In Trnopolje it began with armbands. Like the Jews of Nazi Germany, Muslim residents of the northern Bosnian village were ordered to wear distinguishing armbands. Then on 9 July 1992 uniformed soldiers hammered on the Elezovics' door. Edin and Emir had been working in the fields all day. Their mother Suvada was making coffee for them. The boys, who were in their early twenties, were dragged out of the house and marched with other Bosniak males to the village school. An hour later two more soldiers gathered up Suvada and the other Bosniak women – some of whom were pregnant, others carrying babies – and ordered them to the school as well.

'Nobody could have believed this would happen in a quiet village so far from the front line,' said Muharem, who had been away at the time working as a painter in Slovenia. 'We were simple farmers. It was summer. It was the time to be in the fields.'

The school and adjoining community centre had been transformed into an internment camp. It was enclosed by wire fencing, including barbed wire, and surrounded by machine gun emplacements. Suvada and the other women were imprisoned for three days then crammed into cattle cars and sent to Doboj from where they had to walk across the front line to Bosniak territory. The men – including her two boys – were trucked to Keraterm, a nearby concentration camp run by Serbian paramilitaries and the embryonic Republika Srpska, a self-declared Serbian republic within Bosnia.

66   Here, as at Omarska and Manjaca, inmates were tortured, raped and
      beaten with steel cables and baseball bats. Two weeks later over two
      hundred Bosniak men were packed into three buses and driven to
      the Koricani cliffs, an isolated spot near Mount Vlasic. At the edge
      of a ravine the prisoners were shot and pushed over a one-hundred-
      metre high precipice. Police officers, who had gone out of their way
      to devise the execution, fired on the corpses and threw grenades at
      them before leaving the area. To this day less than a quarter of the
      victims of this massacre have been found and identified. Edin and
      Emir remain among the missing.

      After the end of the war Muharem and his wife returned to Trno-
      polje.
        'When we came back, the house didn't exist,' he said, his tone
      controlled and measured. 'All our possessions – even the door
      frames and windows – had been stolen. I know the man who sold
      the roof tiles and the farmer who has my trailer.'
        'A Serb neighbour found three of our photographs of the boys in
      the debris,' volunteered Suvada in an attempt to leaven the accusa-
      tions. 'She kept them for me.'
        But the same neighbour may well have kept other looted items.
        'Coming home was a matter of the heart,' explained Muharem,
      dragging on his cigarette. 'I have no argument with any Serb in the
      village.'
        But the Elezovics do have an argument with the authorities.
      More than 17 years after the event, no serious investigation to
      locate the missing bodies has been undertaken by the government.
      On behalf of the Elezovics and other families the Swiss Advocacy
      Center – TRIAL (ACT) has lodged applications before the European
      Court of Human Rights.

At the International Criminal Tribunal for the former Yugoslavia, Darko Mrda, a member of the police 'intervention squad' who helped direct the buses to Mount Vlasic, has been convicted of murder and inhumane acts and sentenced to 17 years' imprisonment. Meanwhile in Sarajevo the trial is underway against eight former members of the 'Public Safety Station' who also committed crimes at the Koricani cliffs.

'I've been attending that trial,' revealed Muharem. 'During a break I approached one of the perpetrators and told him, "I want to shake your hand." He assumed I was a Serb and took my hand. I told him, "I don't know if you killed my sons. But I do know that you killed my brother and nephew." The man's mouth fell open.'

Muharem explained, 'I shook his hand to show him what it means to be human. I wanted him to see that I can walk around with my cheek clean. I haven't done anything wrong. But he is already in a wheelchair. God and the people will ensure that justice is done.'

At the far end of the village two teenagers hung around the school and community centre. The older boy Vezir knew that the buildings had been used as a prison because his father had once been held there.

'First it was the House of Culture, then a House of Beatings, now it's a House of Madmen,' he laughed, sitting astride his Ciao moped.

In October 1992 the ICRC had secured the release and evacuation of 1,560 civilian prisoners from the Trnopolje camp. Among the men freed was Vezir's father. He was reunited with his wife who was pregnant with Vezir at the time. Their family was saved. But help came too late for Edin and Emir Elezovic.

Next to the former camp stands a monument dedicated to the

68   soldiers 'who gave their blood to the Republika Srpska'. There is no mention of their Bosniak victims.

Back at home Muharem took off his corduroy cap and turned it in his hands. Not a single picture hung on the white walls around him.

'The two of us are like two lunatics left alone here,' he said, his voice echoing in the empty house.

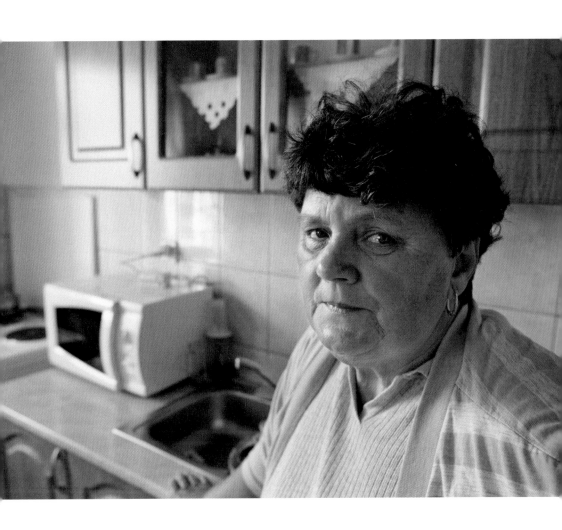

Suvada in her
kitchen. 'Nobody
could have believed
this would happen
in a quiet village,'
said her husband
Muharem.

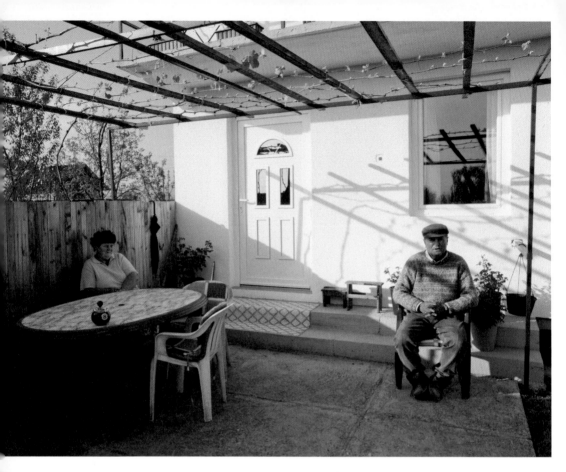

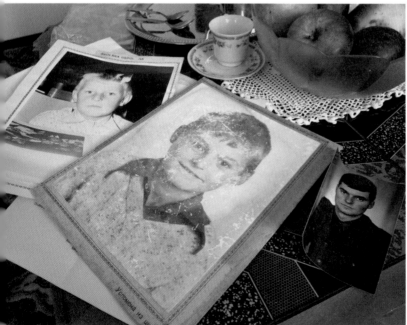

above:
After the war Muharem and Suvada rebuilt the house in which they'd once hoped their sons would raise their own children. 'The two of us are like two lunatics left alone here,' said Muharem.

left:
On a summer evening Edin and Emir Elezovic were taken away from their home by uniformed Bosnian Serb soldiers. Their bodies have never been found.

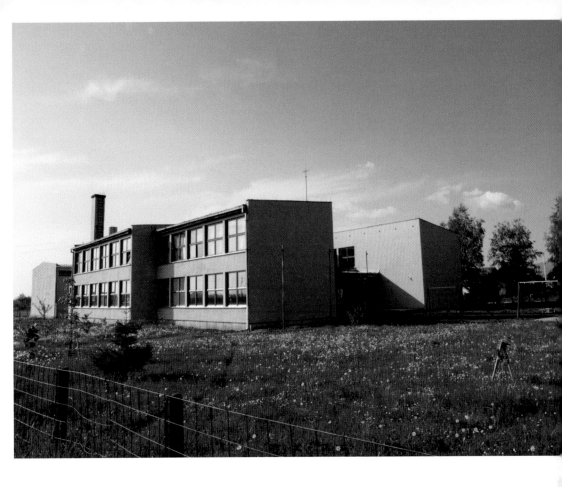

In 1992 Trnopolje
school and adjoining
community centre
were transformed
into an internment
camp, enclosed by
barbwire and sur-
rounded by machine
gun nests.

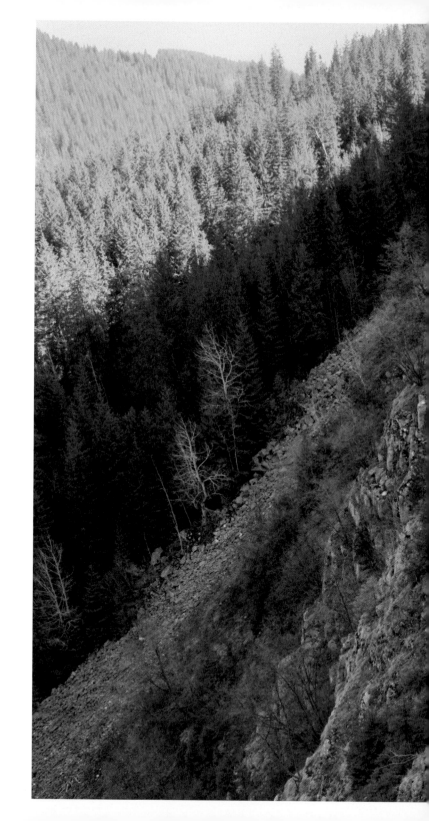

In August 1992 Edin and Emir Elezovic were shot and pushed off the 100-metre-high Koricani cliff with over two hundred Bosniak men. Every year on the anniversary of the massacre, the Elezovics and other bereaved families lay flowers on the cliff edge.

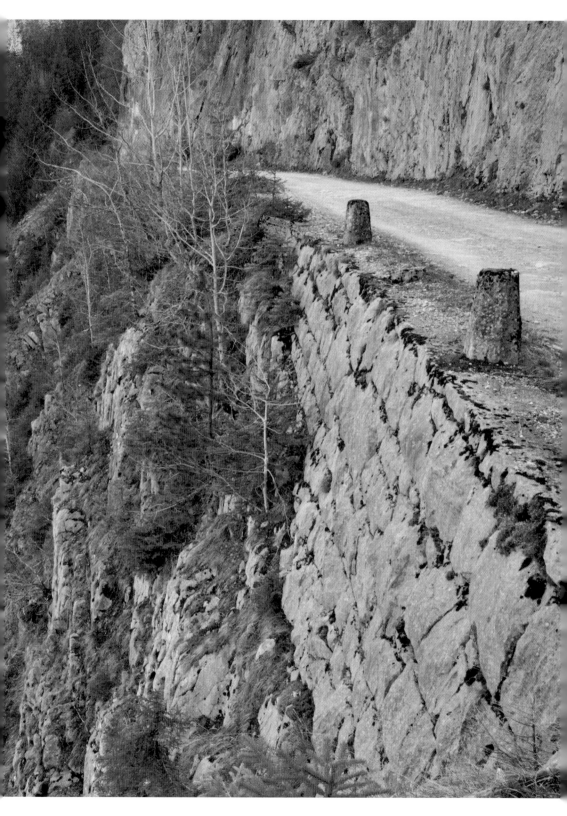

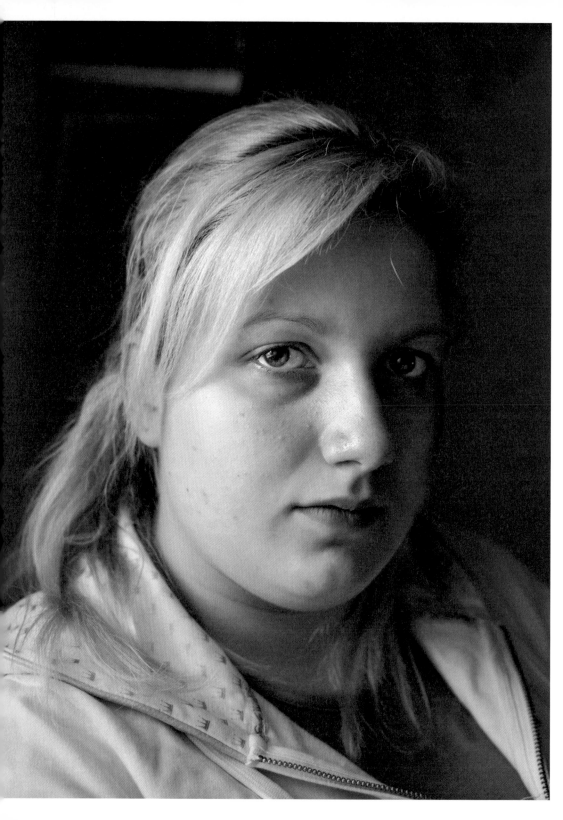

[Senada and Sanda Becirovic]

Sarajevo is synonymous with survival. The Bosnian city resisted the longest siege of a capital in the history of modern warfare. Over three years as many as 500 shells a day were fired on it from Bosnian Serb positions on the steep, surrounding hills. Every spare plot of land was used for growing potatoes or burying the dead. The football stadium's training field became a cemetery. Yet its people were determined to survive, staging a spontaneous Woodstock rock concert in a shattered apartment building, returning to the Markale marketplace the day after a mortar shell killed 68 morning shoppers, publishing the newspaper *Oslobođenje* – Liberation – throughout the war, even as the building was being destroyed floor by floor by tank fire.

Within its barricades some Bosnian Serbs fought alongside the Bosniaks, determined that tolerant, cosmopolitan Sarajevo – which had boasted more mixed marriages than anywhere else in the former Yugoslavia – would not be lost to nationalistic bigots.

Today shell holes still mark the city's fabric and long shadows are cast on the souls of the survivors. Among its many remarkable residents dwells a pretty, soft-skinned teenager with a raw determination to live, no matter what the circumstances.

'A biological father is not necessarily your real father,' stated Mila Jankovic, folding her arms around herself as if in an embrace. 'Your real father is the one who raises you.'

Mila was born Senida Becirovic, a Bosniak. She was 15 months old when her village of Caparde was attacked by local Serb paramilitaries. At the time her father Muhamed was away from home in

Tuzla. Her mother – and possibly her older sister Sanda – were murdered by four soldiers, who then set the family home alight. One of the killers heard Mila's cries. He took pity on the child and rescued her from the flames, giving her to his own mother.

As the father of the poor, Bosniak orphan could not be found, an article appeared in *Politika*, one of the main Belgrade newspapers, asking for help. An elderly, childless couple Zivka and Zivan Jankovic adopted the child, giving her the name Mila. She grew up happily in Belgrade, in the former enemy's capital, with a Serbian name, becoming a Christian, not knowing if any of her blood relatives had survived the war. 'The Jankovics were so good to me that they were like real parents,' said Mila, pushing back her long, bleach blonde hair, a wide, gentle smile on her lips. She wore a white hooded sweater and had painted her nails in softest pink. 'But I knew that I was adopted so I called them grandmother and grandfather.'

In time the Jankovics grew too old to look after Mila and social services took her into care. At the age of 14 she found herself at the SOS Village for orphans at Novi Sad in Serbia.

Out of the blue she was notified that she might have living relatives. She gave a blood sample and two weeks later met her father Muhamed.

'It was so sudden,' said Mila, gripping herself tighter, recalling the shock of reunion after more than 15 years' separation. 'My father came to the SOS Village, along with his fifth or sixth wife. She was a nice German lady and they live together in Düsseldorf. They have another daughter themselves. I recognised something in his face, something familiar, but right away I didn't feel attached to him.'

Mila had been found by her family not because her father had given blood, but because her aunt – along with her mother's five surviving siblings – had opened a tracing request.

'If I was a parent, and I lost my daughter, I would do everything I could to find her. Why hadn't he come looking for me?' demanded Mila, unable to understand why she had been abandoned, forever scarred like her father by the cruelty of war.

'He took me back to the old house where my mother had been killed,' she recalled. 'He had rebuilt it for his retirement but I felt unhappy there. I couldn't stay. He refused to talk about my mother. He wouldn't even admit that she was dead. He tried to take me to Germany. I wouldn't go to him.'

Instead Mila moved to Sarajevo to live with her aunt and uncle, sharing her cousins' room. Here for the first time in her life she saw a photograph of her mother, standing alone, laughing at the camera.

'That was so different. The sight of it moved me heart and soul.'

Mila's mobile sprang to life, its ring tone playing a sugary ditty 'My sweetheart, my honey bunch, you are so dear'. She answered it, making plans for a weekend trip to the country. When she finished she said with shocking casualness, 'I've found the soldier who saved me, and who probably killed my mother. He's in prison for war crimes here in Sarajevo. I've asked for permission to see him.' Many people still live in fear in the western Balkans. To find the soldier Mila had made calls, visited Serbian neighbours in Caparde, even spoken to the man's mother, but no one would help her. All were fearful of retaliation from their own side. So Mila turned to the internet and, after long hours of searching, located him. 'I simply want to ask him for the truth,' she said, rocking herself from side to side. 'I always think about that day. I don't remember it of course but I can't stop myself from imagining it. I need to find out what really happened. I also have to ask if he saved my sister as

well. I believe there's one certainty in life, that truth prevails. Maybe not today, or tomorrow, or even in one hundred years, but one day the truth will be known.'

In a month Mila will turn eighteen. She's planning a big birthday party with dancing – she is crazy about the samba – but she can't decide whether to hold it in Sarajevo or Belgrade.

'It doesn't matter to me if you are Serb or Bosniak. What matters is that we respect each other. I was born into a Muslim household. In Belgrade I went to church and became Orthodox. Now I am with my Muslim family again. All I ask is not to be called Senida for it reminds me of the war.'

Her allegiance is less complicated when she watches handball matches on television with her cousins; Mila supports the Serbian team while the boys cheer on Bosnia.

'I want to go to university, to find a job and to have my own apartment so as not to be dependant on anyone.' Mila laughed again, flashing a wide smile. 'You know, since my childhood I've dreamt of being a journalist. It's the subject I've always planned to study. Then last month I found out that my mother was a journalist before she married my father, and left Sarajevo to live in his closed, little village.'

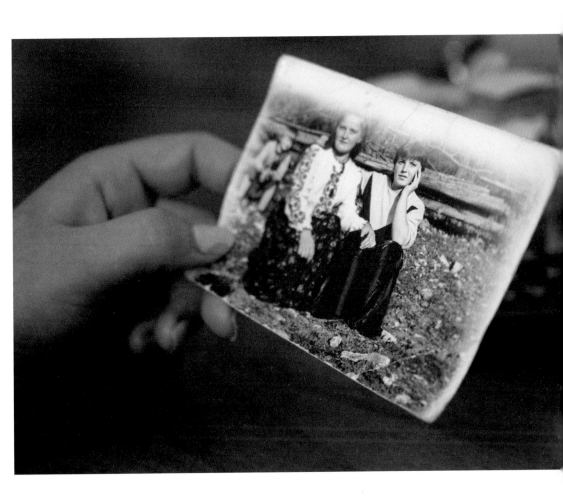

Mila was in her
mid-teens the
first time she
saw a picture of
her mother.

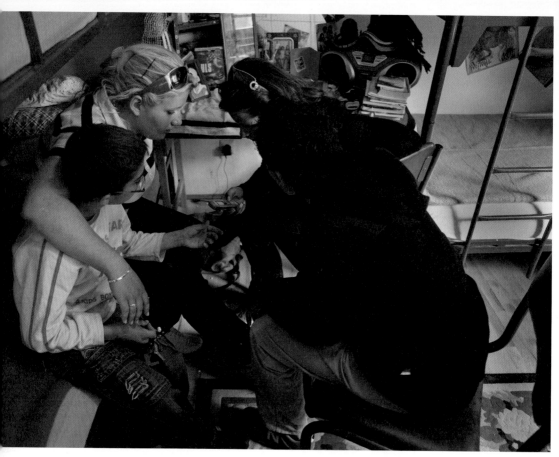

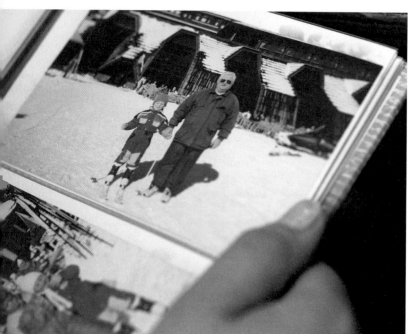

above:
At the age of 14 Mila found herself at the sos Village for Orphans at Novi Sad in Serbia.

left:
Mila was born Senida Becirovic, a Bosniak. After the murder of her mother and disappearance of her father she was adopted in Belgrade, given a Serbian name and raised as a Christian. Here she poses with her adopted father Zivan Jankovic.

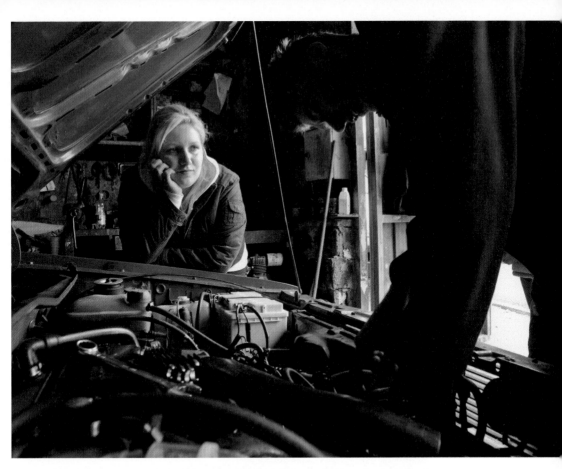

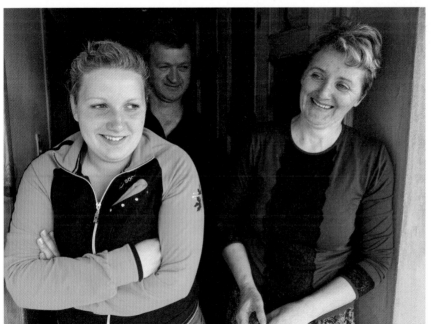

above:
Mila watches her
cousin – who she
calls her brother –
work on his Golf.
'He paints the car.
I paint my hair,' she
laughed.

left:
Twelve years after
opening a tracing
request, Mila was
found by her aunt
and uncle. Until that
point she knew no
blood relative who
had survived the war.

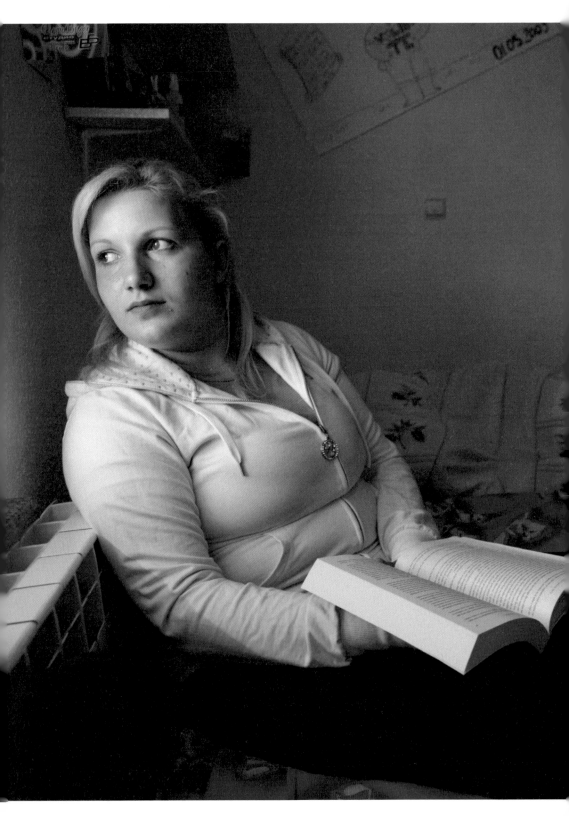

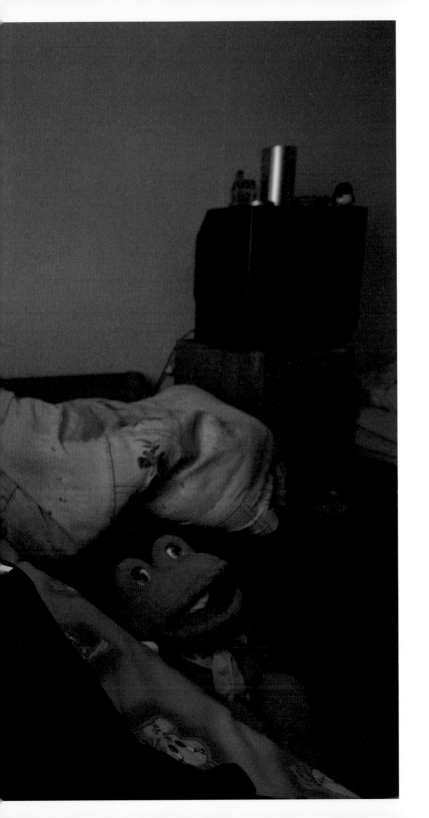

Mila has identified the Serbian soldier who rescued her after allegedly killing her mother. She is determined to ask him if he saved her sister Sanda as well. 'I believe there's one certainty in life, that truth prevails. Maybe not today, or tomorrow, or even in one hundred years, but one day the truth will be known,' she said.

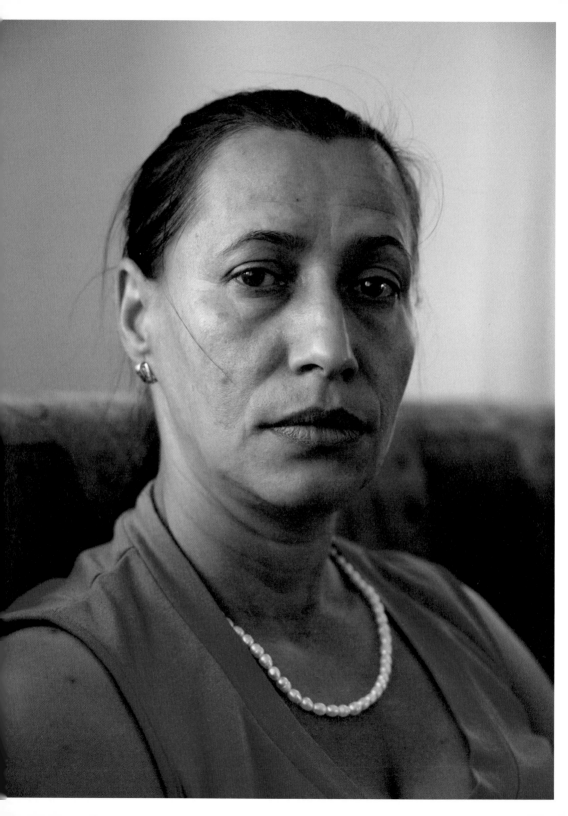

[Mirsad Rizvanovic]

In a pleasant suburban house Kadefa Rizvanovic swallowed her
pills: eleven in the morning, three at midday, three every evening.

'I used to be a sportswoman,' she said. Her long black hair was
pulled back in a severe ponytail, accentuating the narrowness of her
face, exaggerating the width of her mouth and the dark shadows
under her eyes. 'Athletics, handball, I even ran for Bosnia – repre-
senting Srebrenica – at the 1984 Olympics. Now look at me. I'm not
used to staying still.'

Kadefa grew up in a small village outside Bratunac, a Bosnian town
of 30,000 souls on the border with Serbia. A little more than half
the population were Bosniak, and 35% were Serbs. At school in the
fifth grade she met slender, softly-spoken Mirsad Rizvanovic.

'It was love at first sight but we were too shy to tell each other,'
said Kadefa. 'I was very physical, beating up the boys who irritated
me. Mirsad was more sensitive. So we kept quiet and loved each
other in secret.'

At the age of 22 Mirsad and Kadefa were married. He was an elec-
trician. She owned good land which she farmed with her brother
and father. She also worked as a seamstress in nearby Srebrenica,
travelling back and forth by bus every day to make shirts and
trousers for the European market. They built their own house and
in early 1992, when Kadefa found she was pregnant, they bought a
brand new Suzuki jeep. Life was good.

'On April 17 I was coming home on the bus with my friend
Milada. We'd been at school together. We lived next door to each
other. We both worked at the factory in Srebrenica. She seemed

as surprised as me by the Serbian check points that had sprung up along the road. I felt frightened – remember I was Muslim and eight months pregnant by then – so I got off the bus to walk home through the woods. That evening Milada and I had dinner together, as we often did, and she said nothing about it. But she knew. All the Serbs knew what was going to happen.'

When Kadefa went into labour in early May the war had started. She could not reach the hospital because of the fighting so her daughter Sanela was born at home. Two days later the family were forced by Serb paramilitaries to leave the village on foot, abandoning their home, their land and the Suzuki. The journey to Srebrenica – a distance of only ten kilometres – took 22 days, avoiding army patrols, begging for food, sleeping in the open or in barns. Baby Sanela didn't stop crying as Kadefa was too tired and underfed to produce enough milk for her.

'People were naive,' she admitted. 'We knew that there had been wars in Slovenia and Croatia but we never thought it would happen in Bosnia. When fighting did start around Sarajevo we never imagined that it would reach Bratunac. Bosniaks and Serbs had been living together there for years. We trusted each other. So when they started shooting at us we just fled.' She sighed. 'How did I do it so soon after giving birth? Fear does wonders.'

In the Yugoslav wars civilians suffered not only as a consequence of fighting, but because they were explicitly targeted as a tool for the achievement of military and political goals. Simply put, the tactic was to surround a community in a horseshoe formation and to terrorise its population. The civilians would then run in the only available direction and their vacated property would be seized. The Bosnian Serbs needed Bratunac for their siege of Srebrenica. By surrounding the area on three sides, it was they who dictated the direction in which the Bosniaks would run.

87

But there was no escape from Srebrenica. The town had been encircled. The Rizvanovics arrived there with most of the Bosniaks from Bratunac as well as those from Zepa, Visegrad and other neighbouring towns. They escaped the mayhem by taking refuge in Hell, for Srebrenica was a prison camp in all but name. Food was so scarce that people ate grass and tree bark. The family shared a small room with 17 other refugees. Their second child Dino was born during the second year of captivity. In the third year the tens of thousands of starving refugees tried to flee as the Bosnian Serbs began their final attack.

The refugees headed for the town of Potocari, seeking protection within its UN compound. As Bosniak men were being executed on the road and in nearby factories, Mirsad and Kadefa's brother's only chance of survival was to hide in the forest. Mirsad kissed his wife and children and disappeared. Kadefa never saw him again.

'I carried both children. When the shelling started I dropped Dino on the road. I couldn't hear him breathing. I thought he was dead,' she said, trying to staunch the welling tears. Her lips and eyes seemed to swell in grief. 'Mirsad and I had six years together as man and wife, and only one of them was in peacetime.'

After two days in Potocari, with only powdered juice to feed the children, Kadefa was transferred away from the area. In 1996 she opened a tracing request with the ICRC. The following year a mass grave was excavated at Pilice. A total of 42 mass graves were later uncovered in the area. As well as the thousands of skeletons, many personal possessions were unearthed. In one of the Books of Belongings – albums of personal items unearthed with the remains of the dead – Kadefa recognised a photograph of a man's belt and a pair of torn trousers, stitched in the way she had once repaired

88   Mirsad's trousers. But she refused to accept his death until six years later when a DNA match identified his bones.

'Until that day I'd kept hoping that he was alive and imprisoned in Serbia. But when I received the phone call I could not hope any more.'

Sanela and Dino, her shy and troubled teenagers, came into the living room. She embraced them and said, 'Dino is so much like his father. Mirsad taught himself the accordion. Dino plays the guitar. Both of them like cooking, which is unusual for men. Mirsad loved to bake cookies.'

She possesses only two photographs of her husband; the first was a snapshot of the family taken in Srebrenica, the second an enlargement of his passport photograph.

'Sanela told me she dreamt about Mirsad one night, and asked me to make a blow up. He looks so young in it.'

Kadefa began to cry and Dino left the room. He could not bear to see his mother suffer. In a cruel final twist she has been diagnosed with thyroid cancer. Two operations seem to have arrested its spread but the doctor insists that she must rest as often as possible. Around her in the living room were dozens of clocks, some running, some not. 'I've stopped believing in people, in the good human soul,' she said at the front door. I only believe in God now.' She hesitated before adding, 'It's my big wish to see my old friend Milada again. To face her and to say, "Why didn't you tell me?"'

Then she closed the door of her ordinary suburban house.

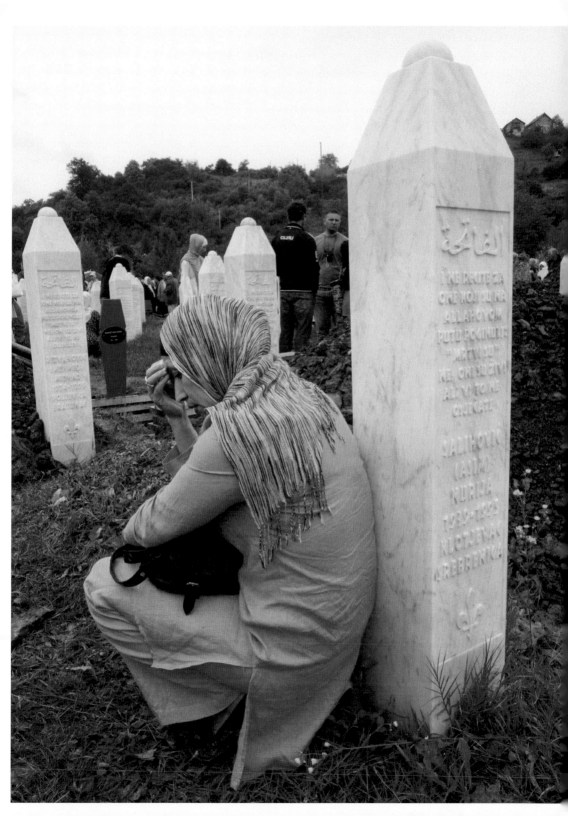

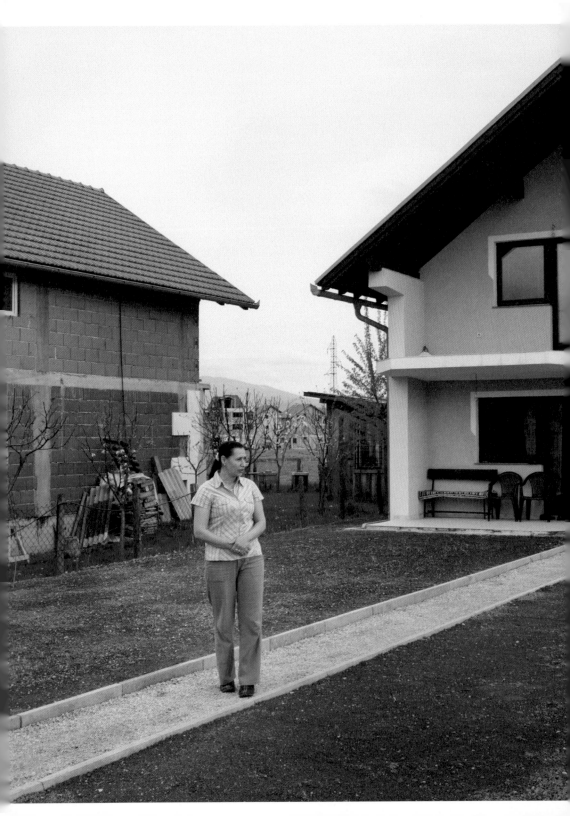

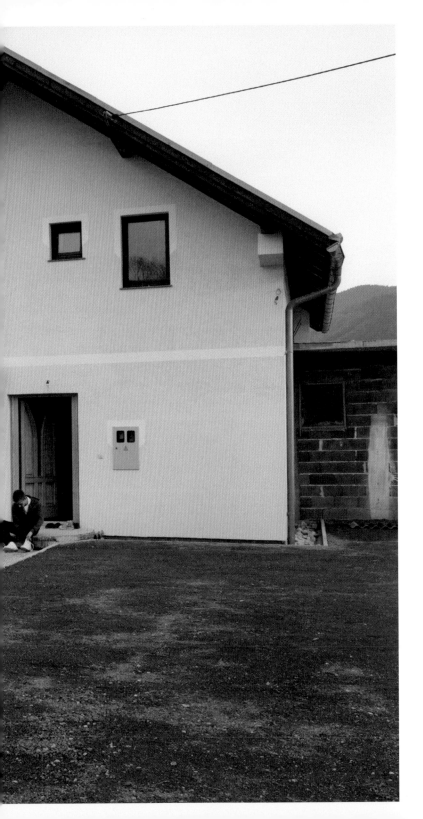

previous page:
Khadefa's husband,
Mirsad Rizvanovic,
is buried at the
Srebrenica-Potocari
Memorial and Ceme-
tery to Genocide
Victims, alongside
thousands of other
men, women and
boys killed in the
Srebrenica massacre.

left:
Kadefa Rizvanovic
at her house on the
outskirts of Sarajevo.
Her family home
in Bratunac was
destroyed (see pages
94–95).

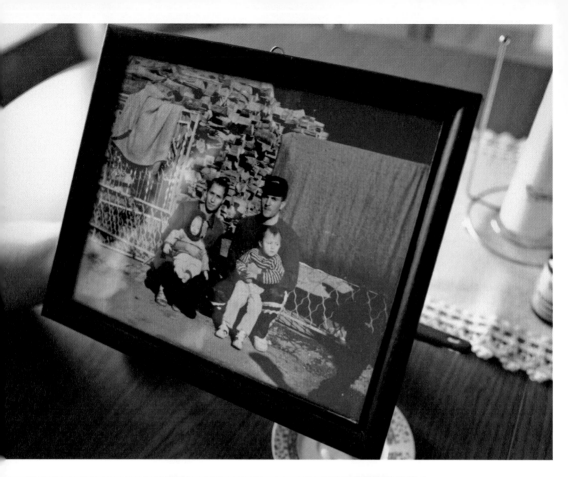

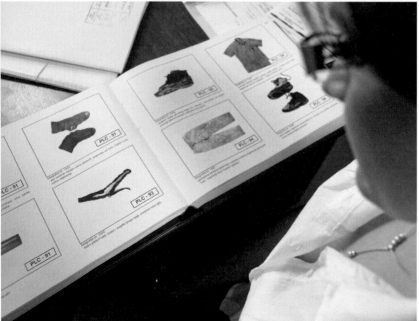

above:
Mirsad and Kadefa
with their children
Sanela and Dino in
Srebrenica during
the second year of
the siege. 'Mirsad
and I had six years
together as man and
wife, and only one
of them was in peace-
time,' said Kadefa.

left:
The Books of
Belongings, albums
of personal items
unearthed with the
remains of the dead,
are published by the
ICRC. In one of them
Kadefa recognised a
photograph of her
husband's belt and
torn trousers.

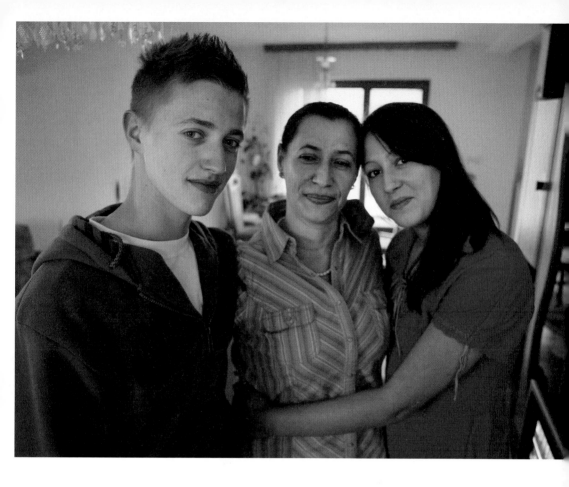

Kadefa lives with her children Sanela, 17, and Dino, 15. She believes that dog food which she ate while pregnant in Srebreni-ca created 'bad blood' that damaged Dino's eyesight.

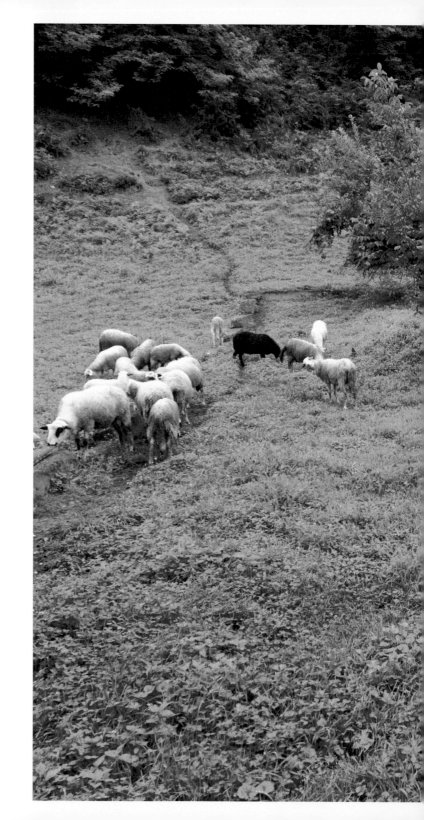

Kadefa buried her kitchen utensils and crockery under their garage so that the family could eat a meal on returning home. The house was razed to the ground and they never came back.

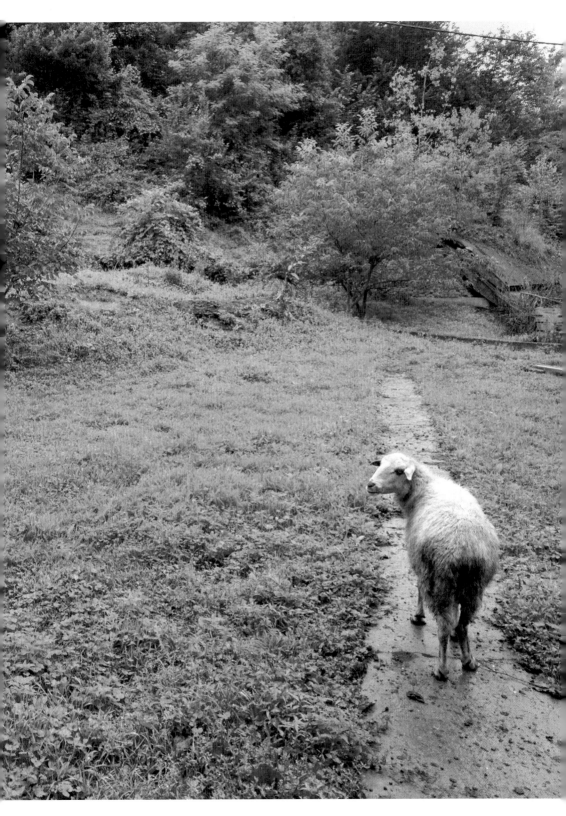

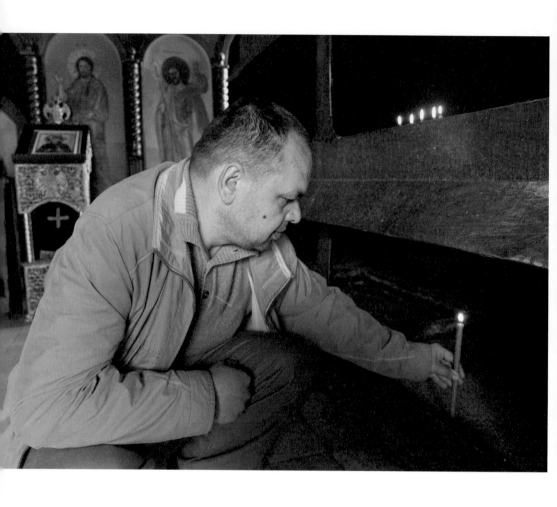

[Svetko Kaurin]

Steep, twisting roads climb towards the clouds. White water streams churn and froth between pine-clad hills. The Ozren mountains appear to be the most peaceful place in all the Balkans. But amidst their quiet alpine meadows are unmarked graves, unexploded mines and bloody secrets. Once, the Bosnian mujahideen, the foreign volunteers who came from north Africa, the Near and Middle East to fight alongside the Muslims, had hidden in its villages.

'We called it chest-to-chest fighting,' murmured Rade Kaurin, a pacing bear caged in a tiny apartment in Banja Luka, the second largest city in Bosnia and Herzegovina. His two small boys tumbled across his lap and through his enormous hands. Washed babygro sleepsuits and rompers dried at the window. 'It was like wrestling in a pot. I never believed I would live through those days.'

During the Bosnian war, softly-spoken Rade was conscripted twice, first into the regular Yugoslav Army then into the Bosnian Serb army. His father Svetko was also called up and posted to the same unit.

'We were sent to the Ozrens to defend the front line. The situation was critical there. Many of our comrades were killed,' he whispered with deceptive calm. 'My father and I stood arm-to-arm throughout the fighting.'

The mountains were important to the Serbs for both symbolic and strategic reasons. Medieval monasteries had long been established there and a small number of Serbian troops – among them Rade and his father – could tie down three whole corps of Bosniak soldiers.

98

At the end of August 1995 Rade's father was transferred to
another unit which was encircled and captured. Svetko was taken
to Kesten and then Gostovici where, according to Rade, the mujahideen offered to release him and the other prisoners on payment of
500 Deutschmarks per head. The Bosnian Serb authorities did not
pay the ransom and Svetko vanished.

Ten weeks later the war was ended by NATO bombing and the
Dayton Accord. Rade began to hunt for his father. He hounded the
military authorities and the Ministry of the Interior. He followed
up rumours that Serb soldiers were imprisoned in Tuzla. As soon as
the technology was available, he gave a blood sample to the ICMP
in the hope of a DNA match. In Gostovici an excavated mass grave
was uncovered but all the remains had been spirited away to other
secret sites. Later some fifteen bodies were found in a secondary
grave on a nearby river bank. They were identified as those of men
having belonged to Svetko's unit. But there was no sign of Svetko
himself. His widow died embittered by the government's failure to
find her husband.

Rade became an active member of the leading Bosnian Serb
family group, the Association of Killed and Captured Soldiers and
Missing Civilians of the Republic of Srpska. His responsibilities
included reading the proofs of its magazine *Hopes*. While checking
one article a small photograph caught his eye. The picture showed a
captured Bosnian Serb soldier with an agonised face surrounded by
masked men.

'I was 100% sure it was my father. I made copies of the photograph and sent them to my relatives. My sister confirmed that it was
him.'

The source of the image was found by the magazine's editor

and the Tracing Commission. A propaganda video had been made
by the mujahideen about the Ozren conflict. The tape ended with
the execution of Rade's father. On camera he was beheaded with a
curved sword.

'I didn't own a video player then so I watched it with my godfa-
ther,' Rade said, stifling his anger. 'We played it over and over again.
I don't know how many times. Afterwards I gave the tape back to
the Commission. I didn't keep a copy.'

Since the war Rade, who trained as an agricultural engineer, has
had difficulty finding work. He looks after his boys while his wife –
an English teacher – is away at school. He laughs almost too easily,
shifting his jacket across his shoulders as he speaks, lighting yet
another Ronhill cigarette. The former concierge's apartment where
his family live consists of only two small rooms. At night he and
his elder boy sleep around the kitchen table. His wife and the baby
sleep in the cramped living room.

'One day I will tell my sons what happened to their grandfather,'
he said. 'My first boy is named after him. But I will wait until they
are ready.'

When not looking after the children he lumbers into the Tracing
Commission, asking for news of newly-discovered graves. 'I believe
that my father's body is somewhere in those mountains, either lying
in the woods or buried in a grave. I am sitting and waiting until it is
found.'

Rade provided information to the Hague Tribunal investigators
during the trial and conviction of the Bosniak General Delic.

'I wish that our leaders – and the authorities – could overcome
the barriers that divide the Balkans,' he said in a placid tone, suck-
ing hard on his cigarette, pursing his boxer's lips. 'I believe that

100   honest people from all sides of the conflict are ashamed, not only for what happened in the war, but for causing such terrible suffering for the families of the missing.'

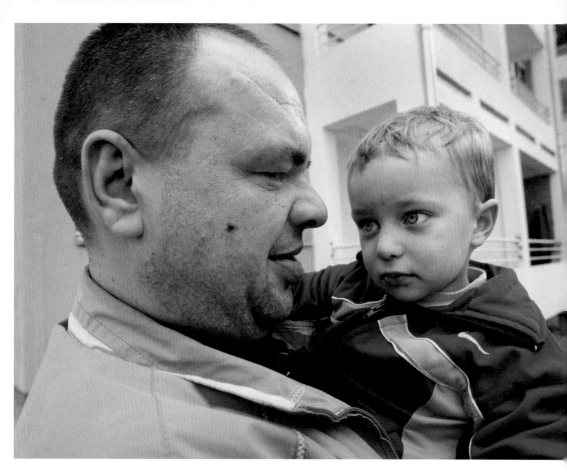

above:
Rade's elder son
Svetozar, aged two,
is named after his
father Svetko. 'One
day I will tell my sons
what happened to
their grandfather,'
said Rade. 'But I will
wait until they are
ready.'

left:
A frame Rade found
in a Bosnian muja-
hideen propaganda
video in which a
Serbian soldier –
allegedly Rade's
father – is beheaded.

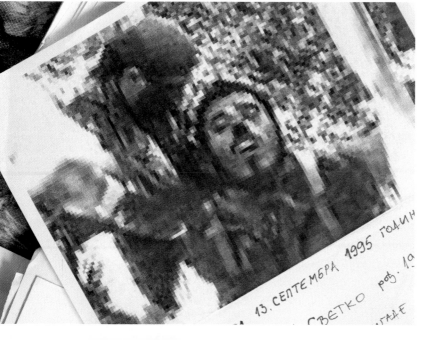

13. СЕПТЕМБРА 1995 ГОДИН

СВЕТКО рођ. 1

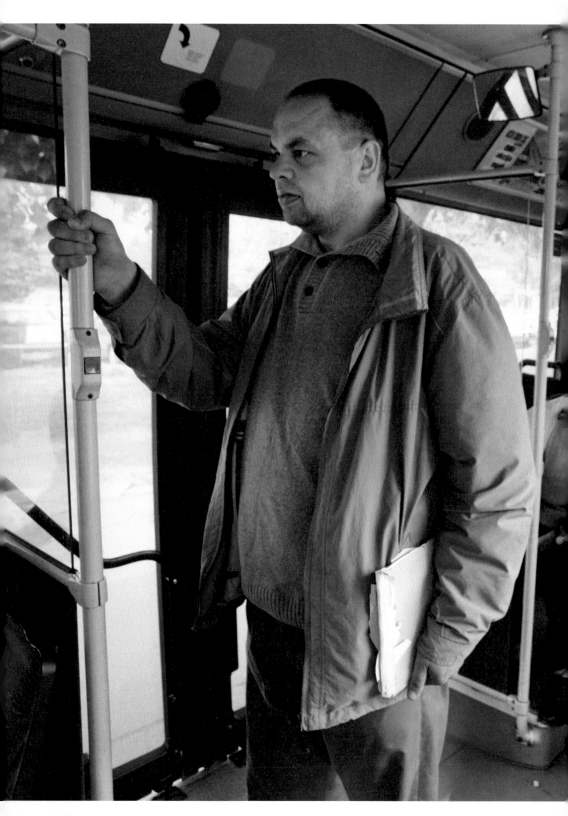

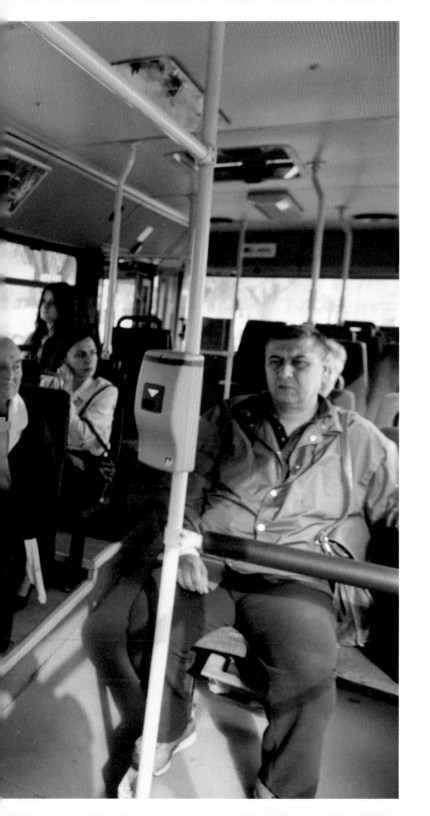

Once a week Rade
travels to the Tracing
Commission for
news of newly-
discovered graves.

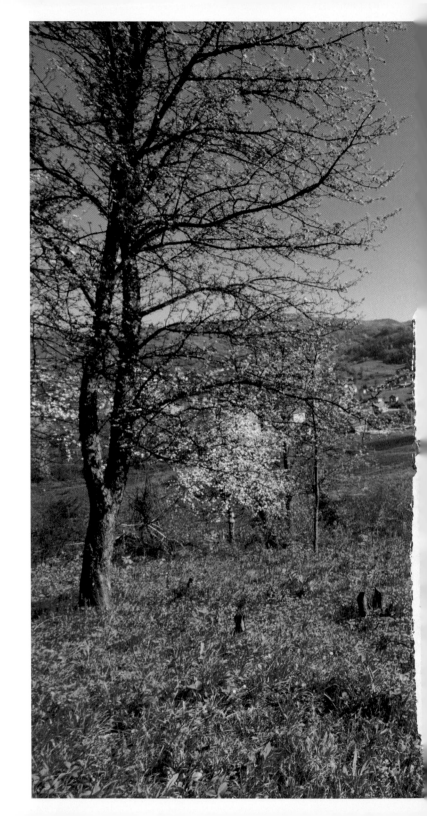

Svetko was held prisoner and allegedly executed in Gostovici, a headquarters of the Bosnian mujahideen in the Ozren mountains.

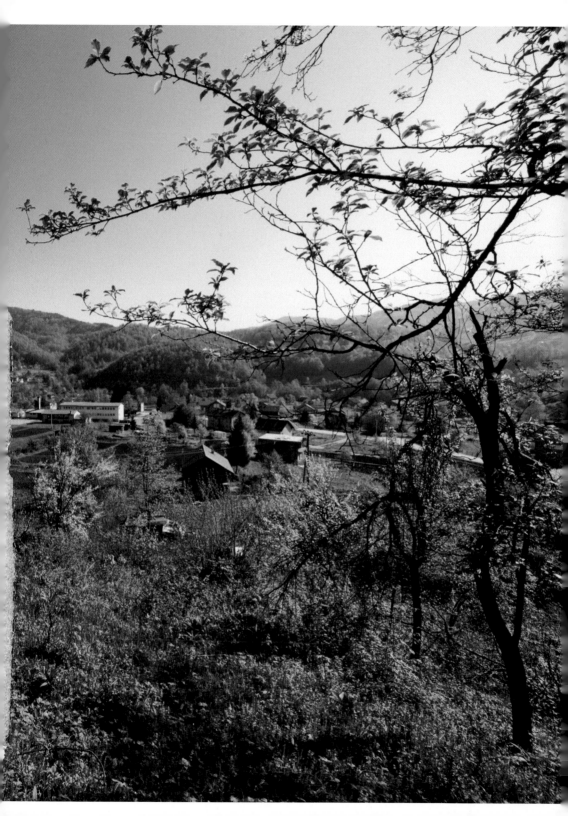

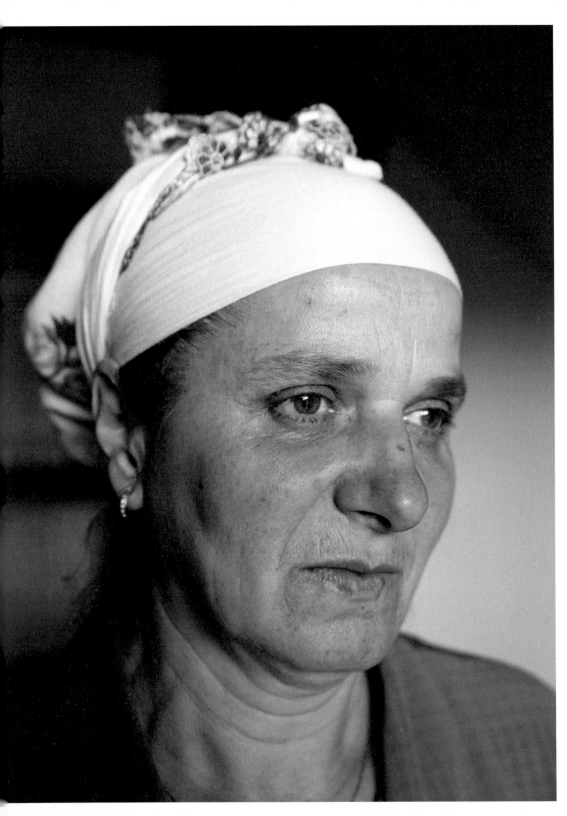

   [Abdulah, Almir and Azmir Mehmedovic]

In villages around Srebrenica almost every other building was a
ruin. Amidst the devastation rose busy Orthodox churches and
deserted mosques without a congregation. Vast cement crosses
squatted on main streets. Blue beehives and slender white gravestones mounted the hillsides. Above them spread a ghost town of
torched and vacated houses, their roofs collapsing, their windows
open to the elements. Among them was a pretty little garden of
yellow and red tulips, and a single restored home. Beside it stood
two young evergreens.

   'My youngest boy Azmir planted the trees,' said Dzidza Mehmedovic, 'one for him and one for his brother. Every morning I look
at them growing taller and stronger.'

The Balkans contain a reservoir of tragedy but in few places is that
reservoir as deep as in Srebrenica. The town in eastern Bosnia was
besieged for much of the 1992–95 conflict. Tens of thousands of
Bosniaks were trapped in it. Despite being declared a demilitarised
'safe area' under the care of the United Nations Protection Force
UNPROFOR, it was eventually overrun by Bosnian Serb forces.

   'Before the war I was a happy woman. I woke up and had
something to look forward to in my day,' said Dzidza, speaking
with fierce energy. 'But if I had known what was going to happen,
I would never have had children.'

   In the days following the takeover of Srebrenica, the Bosnian
Serb Army planned and implemented the execution of almost 8,000
men and boys.

   'My husband Abdulah and our sons tried to escape through the

forest,' said Dzidza. 'Almir was wearing khaki jeans and a white shirt. Azmir had on old black trousers and carried his clean jeans in a plastic bag. I gave them bread. We had no other food to eat.'

Like most of the women Dzidza was evacuated to Tuzla and then Sarajevo. But unlike them, and against the advice of her friends, she was determined to return to Srebrenica.

'I felt that if I came back I would learn the truth faster,' she raved. Her white head scarf was edged in green and yellow flowers. 'I also believed that my family would return to me. I knew it was irrational but I had to do it.'

The Serbs who had occupied her house stole her furniture and threw her personal possessions onto the rubbish tip. On her return Dzidza combed through the tippings and found Almir's last class photograph, Azmir's water-stained school exercise book and a single marble.

'I worked for weeks to put the house back together,' she said. 'The morning after I'd finished, I heard a voice call, "Mama!". I ran outside. I ran up the lane. Of course there was no one there.' She hurried on, 'I used to worry about my boys slipping on the snow, or falling down and grazing a knee. How could all that be taken away from me?'

Dzidza had leafed through a Book of Belongings.

'I stared at one photograph after another,' she recalled, 'and I prayed to God not to recognise anything, even though I wanted to end the uncertainty.'

Later, when DNA became a method for matching living relatives to recovered bones, she gave a blood sample to the ICMP. Twelve years after the massacre she finally received news of her family's fate. The skeleton of one of her sons had been identified, but because the boys had been so close in age it proved impossible to determine

if it had belonged to Almir or Azmir. Of her husband only a single
tibia remained.

'How can I bury a single bone?' wailed Dzidza. 'How can I bury a son not knowing if it's Almir or Azmir? The greatest joy in life is to have a child. The greatest tragedy is to have him or her taken away.'

Dzidza is a member of the Srebrenica Mothers' Association which provides support for women still searching for missing family members whose bodies were dispersed in as many as a hundred mass graves.

'Those people who were in uniform on the day of the genocide, I know them well. In town they either act as if they don't recognise me or insult me by calling me a liar, saying that the Potocari Memorial is not true. Not true!' she cries. 'There are thousands of graves at Potocari, thousands of men and boys who were killed simply because they had different names.'

The International Criminal Tribunal for the Former Yugoslavia found that the mass execution of Bosniak men and boys constituted an act of genocide. Senior Bosnian Serb army and police officers have been charged and imprisoned. But many individual foot-soldiers who carried out their orders remain free, feeling no regret, expressing no remorse.

Dzidza went on, 'I am a small woman but I am a strong woman. I can fight. I'll do whatever I can to prevent a similar tragedy happening to another mother or child. We must learn that evil does not come alone. One evil deed creates another. If we are to regain the trust of our neighbours, we have to deal with history. We have to know who started this war. I don't want vengeance. I want justice.'

Dzidza is a prisoner, unable to free herself, trapped since 1995 by love for her family and grief. 'There is no happiness in other

people's sorrow. There is no happiness in tears. No one will ever build a happy home in this place again,' she said standing on her balcony overlooking the devastated houses that surround her. 'This is the place I raised my children. Whenever I am away, I want to rush back to be here for them. I know that their remains have been found. But in my heart I still believe that my boys might come home for dinner.'

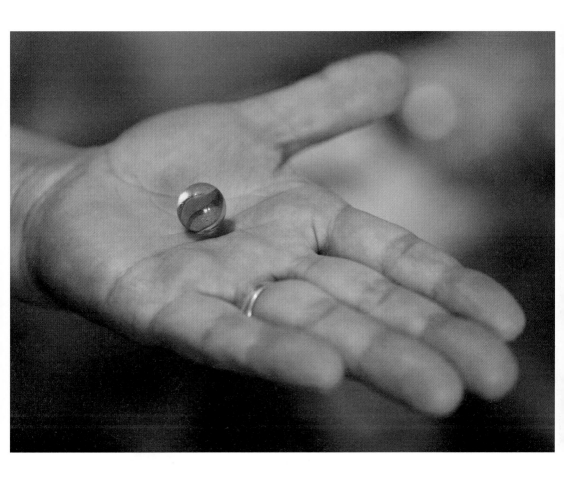

All of Dzidza's
possessions were
stolen, burnt or lost.
On her return home
all she found was
a school exercise
book and one of
her son's marbles
in the rubbish tip.

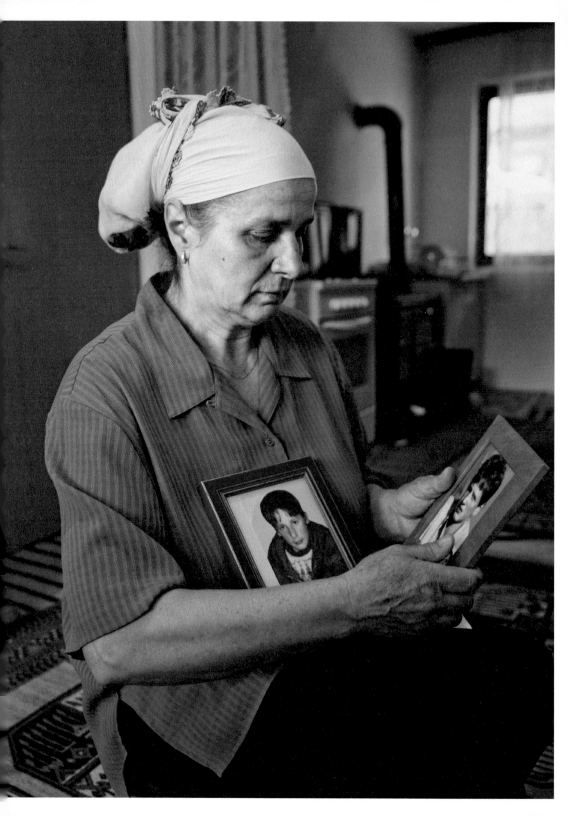

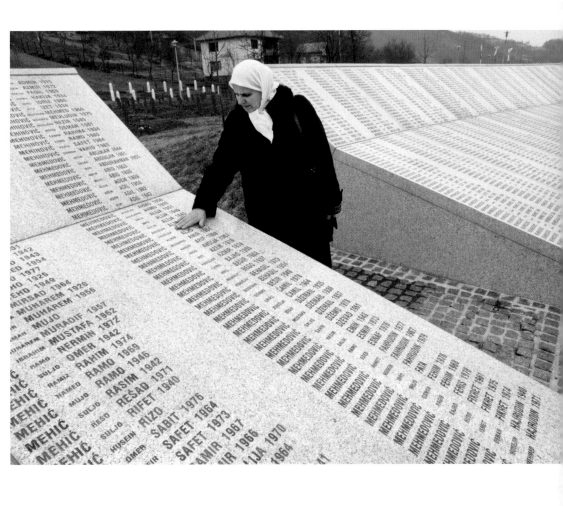

Dzidza's two sons, Almir, 12, and Azmir, 15, went missing along with her husband while attempting to escape from Srebrenica, site of Europe's worst massacre since the Second World War.

Dzidza regularly visits the Srebrenica cemetery. 'I want everyone to come and see the Memorial. To see it as a mirror and look at the ugly image it reflects,' she said.

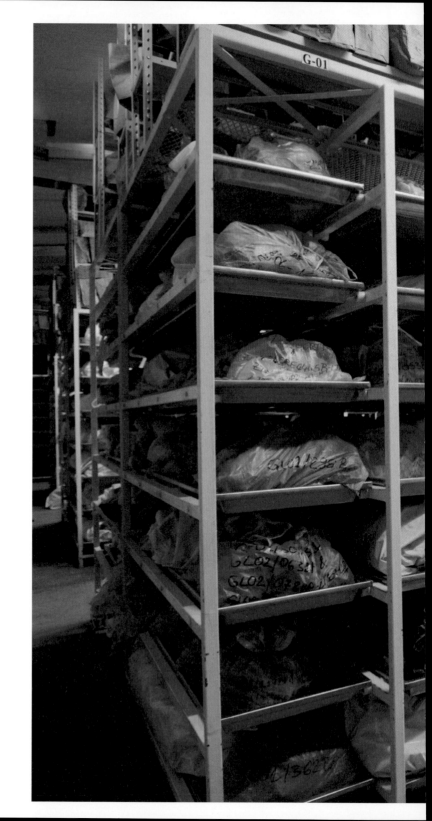

Thousands of
remains recovered
from mass graves
around Srebrenica
await identification
at the ICMP's cold-
storage warehouse
in eastern Bosnia.

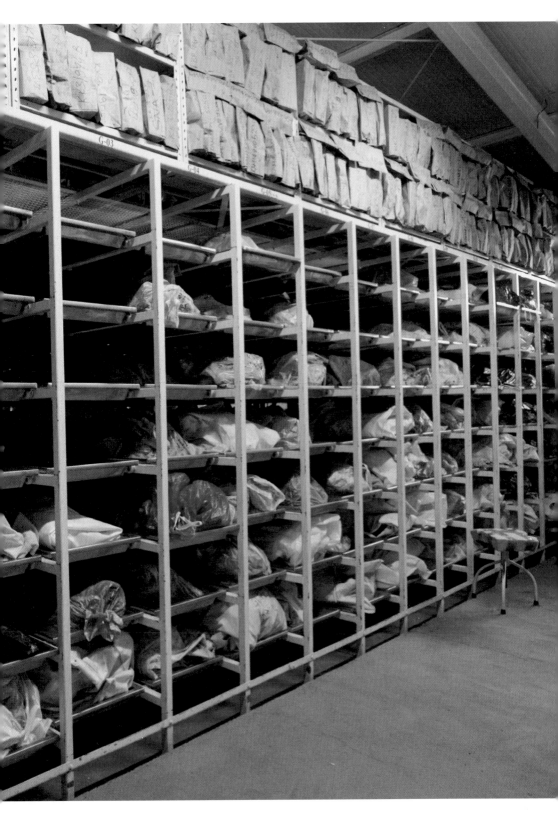

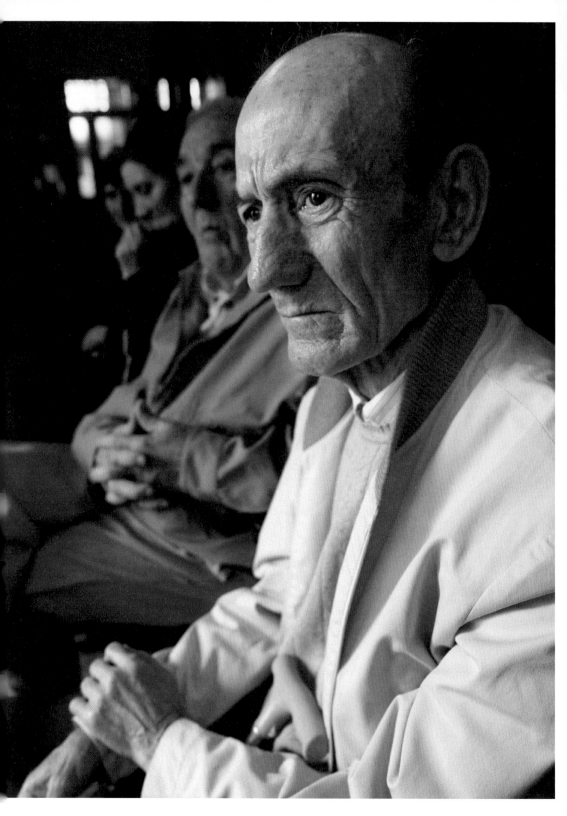

 [Milica Brujic]

All her life Milica Brujic would not leave her home in Tomingaj.
Only death could separate her from it.

Milica lived in a cluster of houses above Tomingaj – or Toma's
Copse – in the Dalmatian mountains. Five hundred years ago Serbs
had been settled there, and in nearby Knin, to guard the borders
of the Austro-Hungarian Empire. Milica grew up to love the high
Dalmatian meadows, the hard winters and far vistas. She fell in
love with a blacksmith from the coast, who built his smithy beside
the family house, and bore seven children. Her hospitality was
renowned in the hills, welcoming guests with glasses of slivovitz
and thick slices of freshly baked bread.

 'We owned 30 sheep, two cows, two horses and two pigs when
I was a boy,' said bone-thin Jovo, her oldest surviving son. 'We never
went hungry. It was a feast when a pig was killed on St. Luke's Day.'

 But the Second World War brought tragedy to their alpine idyll.
Italian and Ustashi troops mined the village and stole the animals.
The Serbian men – including Milica's husband – joined the Partisans. Night after night Milica took the children to hide in the woods,
sleeping in shepherd's huts, returning home when the invaders had
departed.

 'We had no food, not even one egg for Easter,' said her younger
son Slavko, a sprightly septuagenarian with a round healthy face,
neat white hair and down-turned lips which lifted easily into a
smile. 'Once she begged a little flour from the mill and baked us a
beautiful loaf. But the Partisans happened to pass by and snatched
it from our mouths.'

 Then in 1944 Milica heard an explosion in the garden. Her sec-

ond son had picked up a landmine. It had exploded in his hands.

'The loss changed her forever,' said Slavko. 'She became a different person: nervous, aggressive and unsociable.'

At the end of the war Milica's husband was given a plot of good land in Tito's wealth redistribution programme. But Milica refused to leave Tomingaj – she would not even sleep in another house in the village – so he moved away from her. Most of the children followed as there were few jobs in the mountains.

Slavko settled in Serbia. Jovo trained at Knin agricultural college then found work in Vukovar. The boys travelled back to see their mother every year, installing running water and then electricity in the house. The 1991–95 Croatian war made little impression on isolated Tomingaj. From time to time distant shelling could be heard, but Milica seemed not to notice. She was busy keeping the goats out of the vegetable patch.

In August 1995, when Slavko was visiting his mother, Croatia launched Operation Storm, the largest European land offensive since the Second World War. In a swift and brutal operation, the Croatian army reclaimed seized territory. As the Serbs had done before them, they targeted civilians as part of a campaign of ethnic cleansing. Within three days more than 200,000 Croatian Serbs were fleeing to Banja Luka and Belgrade.

'There were two vehicles left in mother's neighbourhood but no petrol,' said Slavko. 'A friend had a bicycle but she couldn't ride it. She was 87 years old by this time. Perhaps I could have persuaded her to leave Tomingaj if I'd brought my car. I cannot live with the fact that I came without it.'

Slavko heard that a vehicle would arrive to rescue the elderly the next morning. But before the rumour could be confirmed, he and other Croatian Serbs found themselves running to catch up with their retreating soldiers.

'That was the last thing I know about our mother.'			

119

When Jovo learnt that their mother had been abandoned in Tomingaj he wept down the telephone.

'I shouted at Slavko. I cursed him. I had problems of my own. During the siege of Vukovar I had hidden in a cellar for three months – without food or light – and my health never recovered.'

Jovo began to search for her as if possessed, harassing UNPRO-FOR, pestering the local Red Cross and the ICRC with whom he filed a tracing request. On crutches he hobbled almost every day to question Serbian authorities. He travelled to Osijek to give blood for DNA sampling. But the news was always bad.

'Not even a cat had been left alive in our village,' he cried with shocking grief.

Twelve years later Jovo and Slavko travelled by train to Zagreb and took a taxi to the Salata University Hospital. They climbed the stairs to the Institute for Forensic Medicine. They sat in a long corridor with other bereaved families. Behind them on glass fronted shelves was displayed the university's collection of skeletons: human skulls, a crocodile, a hawk.

In time they were called into a wood-panelled office and invited to sit at a long table with a dozen experts, both Croat and Serb. Jovo leaned his cane against the table but it slipped and fell to the floor. Together they heard – relived – the last moments of their mother's life, learning details of the burial place of the then-unidentified body, seeing photographs of the exhumed remains. Jovo's eyes were haunted as he scrabbled for a tissue. The ICMP explained the DNA process, and the certainty of the match.

'At first we didn't understand why her legs were broken,' said Slavko, the hairs of his arms standing on end. 'We were told that her legs had been broken and her skull fractured.'

120

'Why did so many civilians have to be killed?' Jovo begged to know. In the Institute his hands shook so violently that he could not sign his name.

Only in death could Milica be moved away from her beloved mountains.

'We were frightened to go back to Tomingaj. So we decided to bury her in Serbia, in a decent place with her grandchildren nearby,' said Jovo.

The old brothers, who have remained more like sons than husbands or fathers, now visit her on the flat Vojvodina plain. They kiss her gravestone portrait and stroke her marble cheeks.

'Everything was destroyed but at least we know where to find her now,' said Jovo, weeping openly. 'Our mother was the greatest love of my life.'

His grief was so intense that it suggested something remained unspoken. In much of the Balkans people are victims of their emotions, not only because of the extent of their trauma, but because of a knowledge of the history of revenge and of the dark depths of Balkan secrets.

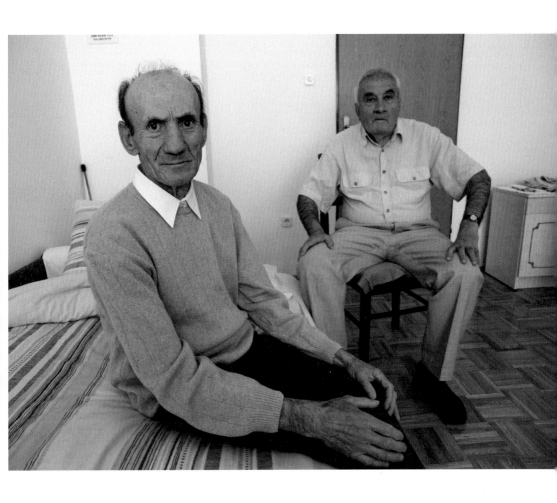

Brothers Jovo, left, and Slavko Zarak at home near the Croatian-Serbian border. 'Can you imagine the feeling of someone sitting on your chest? That is how we felt for twelve years. Twelve years!' said Slavko, recalling the agony before his mother's remains were identified and returned to them.

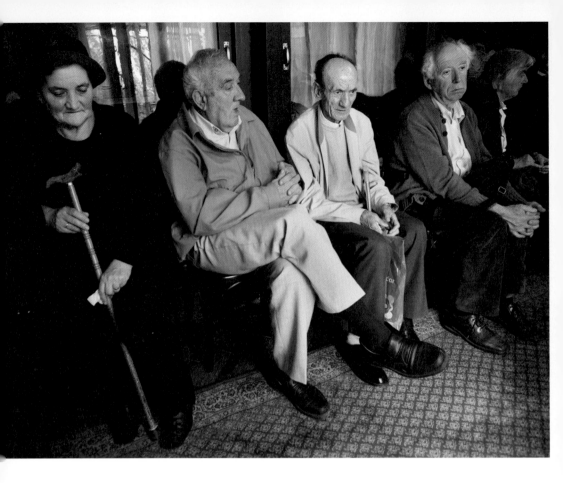

Jovo and Slavko wait
– alongside other be-
reaved families – at
the Zagreb Forensic
Medical Institute
for an identification
session at which they
will receive death
and DNA certificates
as well as any recov-
ered belongings.

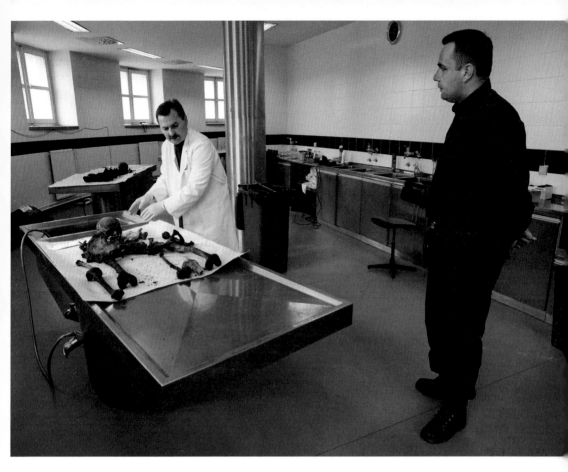

above:
In a Zagreb forensic laboratory skeletons are prepared before being returned to families for burial. Families are invited to view them but are usually advised against doing so.

right:
Milica Brujic's death certificate states the cause of death as unknown.

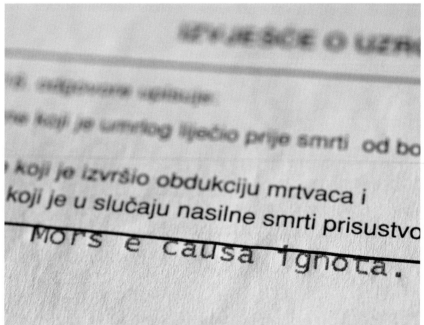

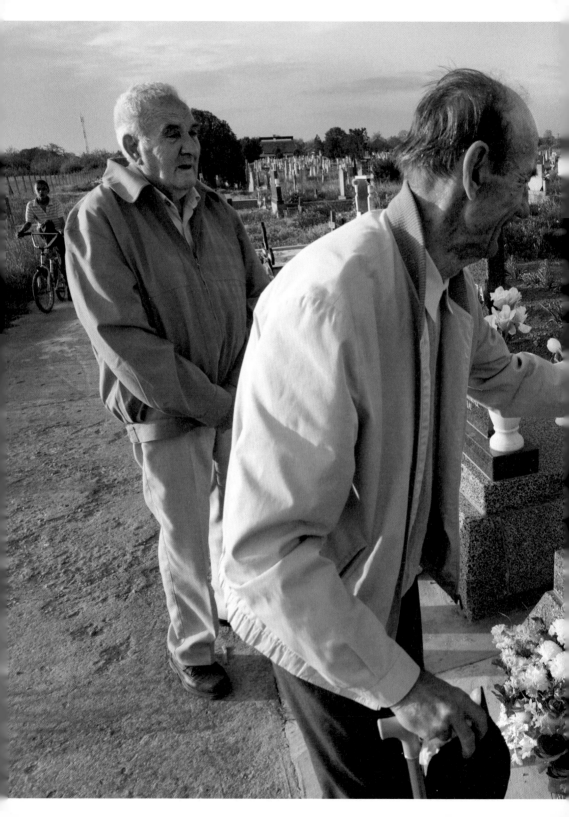

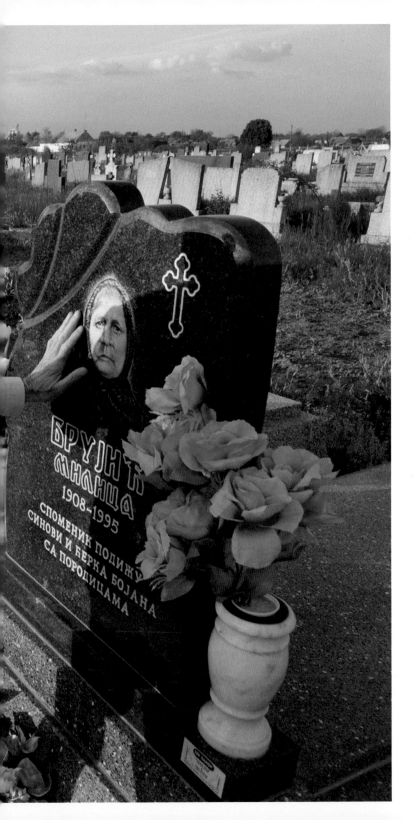

Jovo, right, and
Slavko Zarak grieve at
their mother's grave
on the Vojvodina
plain in Serbia, far
from the Croatian
mountains which
she loved.

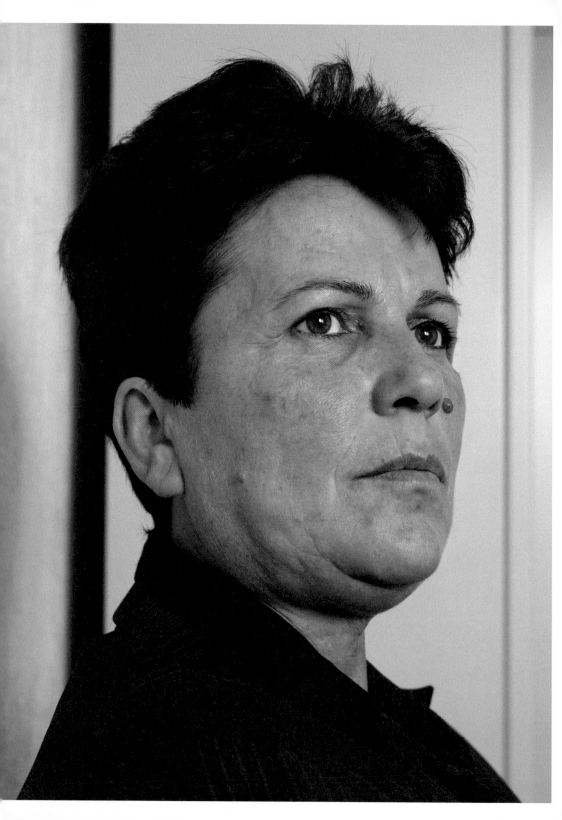

     [Sheremet Ismaili]

'I went back to Kralan right after the war,' said Sevdije Ismaili,
dressed in a stylish black suit, wearing no make-up. 'I saw bullet
holes on the garage walls. I saw scorched patches of ground.
I found burnt jackets stinking of petrol. In an old horse cart were
identity cards, key chains and jaw bones. In the long grass I saw the
silhouette of a body, the grass having not grown underneath it.'
She stubbed out her cigarette and added, 'But I recognised nothing
that had belonged to my husband.'

Two months earlier an armed policeman had ordered the Ismaili
family out of their apartment in Kosovo with the words, 'You
wanted NATO, so you will have NATO.'
     Ninety per cent of Kosovars were Albanians who had long
wanted independence from Serbia. But Serbs regarded the prov-
ince as the cradle of their civilization. In 1989 Slobodan Milosevic
ignited the Serb minority's emotions, inflaming national griev-
ances. Over the next ten years Kosovo descended into war. In March
1999 to stop attacks on ethnic Albanians, NATO launched a bombing
campaign on military targets. In response Serbian ground forces
began a systematic expulsion of civilians from Kosovo. Within
weeks at least 800,000 civilians were forced to flee towards neighbouring countries. Thousands of homes were set alight, the rain
pressing the smoke into low, evil clouds that stained the horizon.
For years to come Kosovo would remain the battleground between
two irreconcilable principles: that of a people to self-determination
and of a state to territorial integrity.
     Sevdije, her husband Sheremet and their three children were

trucked with 200 neighbours away from Klina then told to walk to Albania. Sevdije, a strong and attractive 36-year-old, led the column. She sat her youngest son Burim on a relative's tractor along with their suitcase of clothes, bread and family photograph albums. Slowly the tractor pulled ahead and out of sight.

'We reached Kralan and I had never seen such a big crowd. All the fields were packed with people evicted from Klina, from Skenderaj, and from villages all around.'

As many as 20,000 refugees had taken shelter in and around the village, a few finding accommodation in houses and barns, the majority forced to sleep in the open.

'On our third day there the Serbs started shelling us. We tied a white sheet to a stick but they didn't stop shooting. We had to kneel and crawl to surrender.'

The soldiers wore a variety of uniforms. Some disguised their faces with camouflage paint. They separated women, children and the elderly from the men. Sevdije's husband Sheremet was pulled aside. Sevdije stumbled onwards with her eldest son, 13-year-old Naim. Then, just as she thought Naim was safe, an officer sitting inside a military vehicle rapped his knuckles on the windscreen. He ordered his men to seize the boy.

'Tell them I am too young, Mama,' pleaded Naim but a soldier hit him with a rifle butt and shoved him in with the male prisoners.

'The Serbs started firing into the air. I thought they'd shot him. Suddenly I didn't know what I was doing. I stepped away from the crowd. I lost my daughter's hand. I collapsed beside a tree. I was in shock. A neighbour spotted me and picked me up. She didn't let go of me until we reached Albania.'

The column of women and children walked through the night to reach the border. Paramilitaries came out of the woods to rob them, one holding the nozzle of a machinegun at Sevdije's throat until a ransom was paid. Girls dirtied their faces and wore headscarves to avoid rape. A 15-year-old was pushed all the way in a wheelbarrow, having lost her mind when her father was taken away.

'Across the border in Kruma I found my daughter,' said Sevdije. 'But I didn't know what had happened to my husband or my boys.'

Sevdije endured three tortuous days until she received news that Naim was alive, and three long weeks until she learnt that her youngest son who had been carried away on the tractor was also safe.

Naim had survived because his father Sheremet had offered his life for his son's. At Kralan at least 100 young men including Naim had been selected for execution. Sheremet had begged an officer to take him instead. Naim had been released but as he ran away towards the road, Serbian soldiers had raised their guns to shoot him.

'Let him alone,' called the officer, a self-styled demigod in a village of death. 'He is free.'

'It was a little fortune in the tragedy,' said Sevdije.

Later in her office in the Klina Municipal building Sevdije said, 'Today some people still believe that their loved ones are in secret detention places in Serbia. They pay money for information or send gifts through intermediaries, but nothing comes back to them. One family even received a phone call after their son's body had been found and buried. "That is not your son," argued the stranger on the phone. "Send me money and I'll prove that your son still lives."' Sevdije shook her head sadly. Sheremet has been reported missing to half a dozen organisations and blood samples have been given by all his relations. 'But I don't hold out any hope. I don't believe that he is alive.'

Only a few human remains have been found and identified from the Kralan massacre.

Today Sevdije is a Municipal Returns Officer, managing the re-patriation of Serbs who had fled from Kosovo when the Albanians returned, some of whom were responsible for her – and her family's – banishment. But more painful even than that irony is the expectation that Sevdije should mourn Sheremet for the rest of her life.

'We cannot forget those who have been lost. But it's ten years since my husband died. I am 46 years old and still young. I would love to wear make-up and bright colours again. Red is my favourite colour. But one has to be careful how one is perceived.'

As for Naim, whose life was traded for his father's, he is haunted by the guilt. When he was involved in a recent car accident in which two people were killed he said, 'Every place I go, I cause death.'

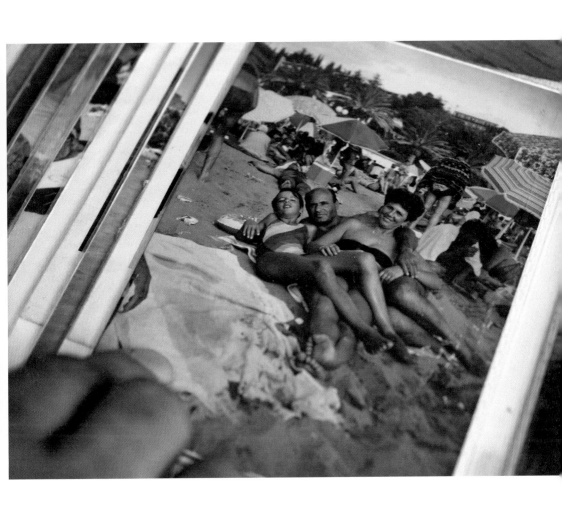

Sheremet and
Sevdije with their
daughter Blerta
on holiday at the
Adriatic.

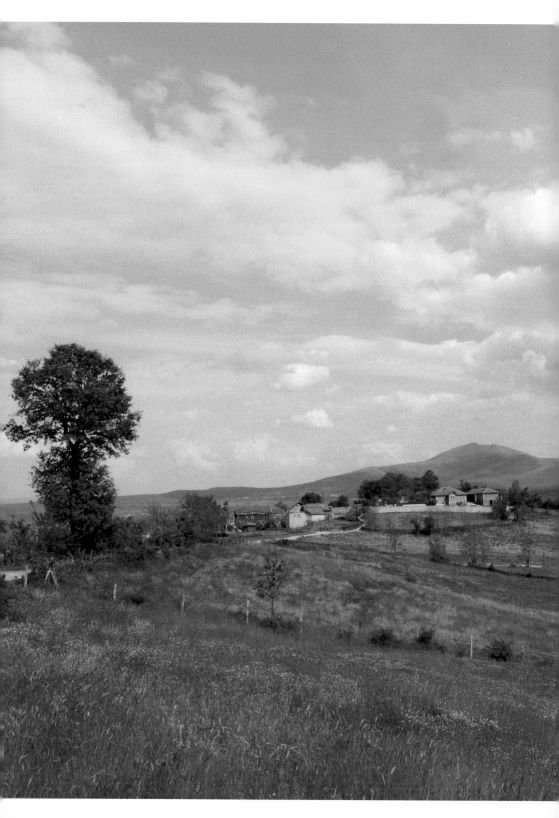

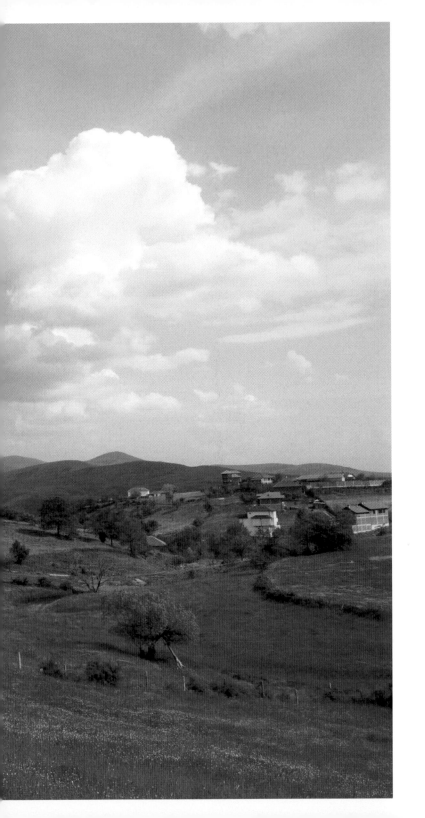

As many as 20,000 refugees took shelter in and around Kralan, the village where Sevdije's husband Sheremet traded his life for his son's.

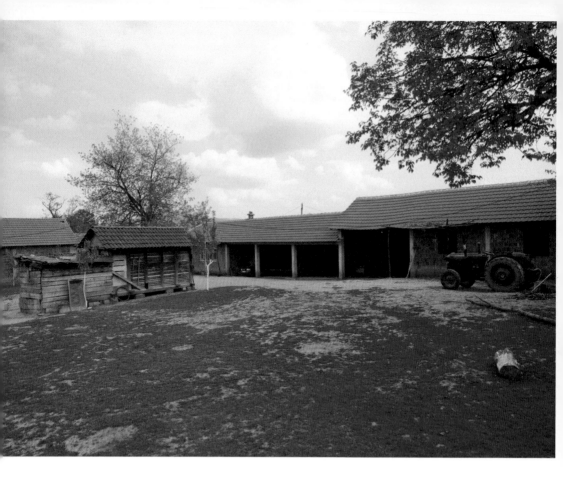

In farm buildings
in Kralan 84 ethnic
Albanians were
executed by Serbian
soldiers and para-
militaries. Grass has
not grown back at
some places where
the dead lay. The
remains of only a
few of the victims
have been found.

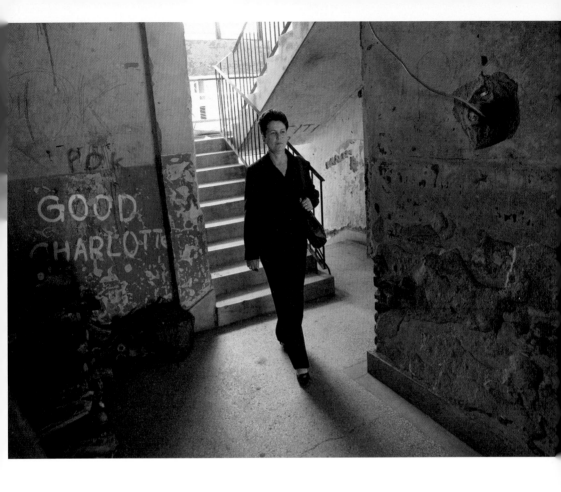

'It's ten years since my
husband died. I am
46 years old and still
young. I would love
to wear make-up and
bright colours again.
Red is my favourite
colour,' said Sevdije.
'But one has to be
careful how one is
perceived.'

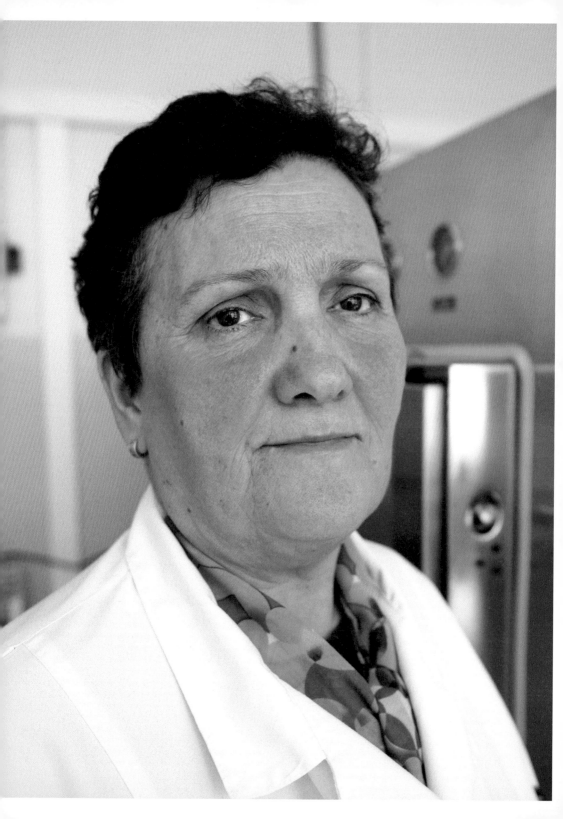

Sanije Recaj
[Bekim Recaj, Basri Tupella and Mehmet Tupella]

NATO aircraft attacked strategic Serbian targets for ten weeks in
1999. Only as the bombs fell did most Kosovo Albanians feel safe,
despite the defiant upsurge of violence against them. The air strikes
forced an end to the massive campaign of destruction and led to the
signing the Kumanovo peace agreement.

On that evening in Mitrovica, a mixed city in northern Kosovo,
Sanije Recaj and her family watched the news, celebrating the end
of the war. As they flicked between BBC World and Euronews, they
were filled with a sense of relief. Then two Serbian police cars and a
military truck drew up outside their Three Towers apartment block.
A moment later a masked man hammered on the door. Sanije
didn't think to pick up the axe which she had kept hidden throughout the conflict because peace had returned to Kosovo. She hardly
worried when her son Bekim, 28, and her two brothers were taken
away.

'Also, I recognised the man in the mask,' she said. 'He lived on
the floor above us. His father and I worked together at the hospital.'

Bekim and his uncles were loaded onto the truck along with
thirteen other residents of the Three Towers. Sanije never saw them
again.

Throughout the war Sanije had continued to work in the
hospital's respiratory department. Bekim had indulged his passion
for basketball, playing with his friends every weekend. During air
raids the family had sheltered in the cellar alongside their Serbian
neighbours. They had attempted to leave Mitrovica, hiring a coach
with other ethnic Albanians on three occasions, paying thousands
of Deutschmarks each time, but they were always turned back by

paramilitaries.

On the night of the abduction, Sanije called the local police station. 'But they knew nothing. I went there the next day, and every day afterwards. As soon as KFOR – the NATO-led Kosovo Force – entered Mitrovica, I pressed charges for kidnapping. Many organisations came to see me, taking notes, asking the same questions over and over again. Almost every day for two years I was shown photographs of clothes and possessions. I did searches on the internet. I paid a lawyer to take on my case. Twice the ICMP took my blood. But no one could give me any useful information.'

Of the 15 men seized that night only three survived, by coincidence one from each of the Three Towers. Among them was Bekim's friend. He later told Sanije – and investigators – that on the night of the abduction the military truck had driven to a railway bridge over the Ibër/Ibar river. The men were marched down the bank and ordered to jump into the fast-flowing water. The police then started shooting at them. The friend claimed that Bekim and one of his uncles managed to swim to the opposite bank and take cover in the bushes. Meanwhile the friend concealed himself in a burnt-out house, eating grass, drinking rainwater, too traumatised to come out of hiding for ten days. He finally emerged expecting to be arrested by Serbian police, finding instead the streets patrolled by French KFOR soldiers.

'We can speculate all day long about how the men were taken to the river, and what happened to them there,' snapped Sanije, at once angry and resigned. 'Maybe they were driven to Serbia. Maybe they were murdered, misidentified and buried under the wrong names, but I don't want to think about that. There are so many possibilities.' She pushed her hands deep into the pockets of her white lab coat, unwilling to expose her emotions again. 'All I want

is clarification of what happened to my son and my brothers.'

139

Five years after the kidnapping, the remains of one brother were located and later identified by the ICMP. The case was then closed by the UN's Office on Missing Persons and Forensics and the body buried in the nearby village of Kcic. The whereabouts of Bekim and Basri Tupella remain unknown to this day.

'There is one person who knows the answer of course. That's my former neighbour, the man in the mask who took them away.'

Since 2004 the ICRC has chaired the Working Group on Persons Unaccounted for in Relation with Events in Kosovo. As the only formal contact between former adversaries, the Working Group has shared information which has led to the identification of gravesites and almost 1,400 human remains. But a further 1,869 individuals – among them Sanije's son and brother – are still missing, their families living in tortuous anxiety, desperate for closure of some kind. The unresolved issue of missing persons fuels resentment between ethnic communities.

Mitrovica remains a divided city, the Ibër/Ibar river a kind of liquid Berlin Wall, the *de facto* border between Albanians and Serbs in Kosovo. Sanije moved away from the Three Towers and now lives on the southern shore but residents on both sides of the river remain shocked by the kidnapping and murders of 9 June 1999, the day the war officially ended.

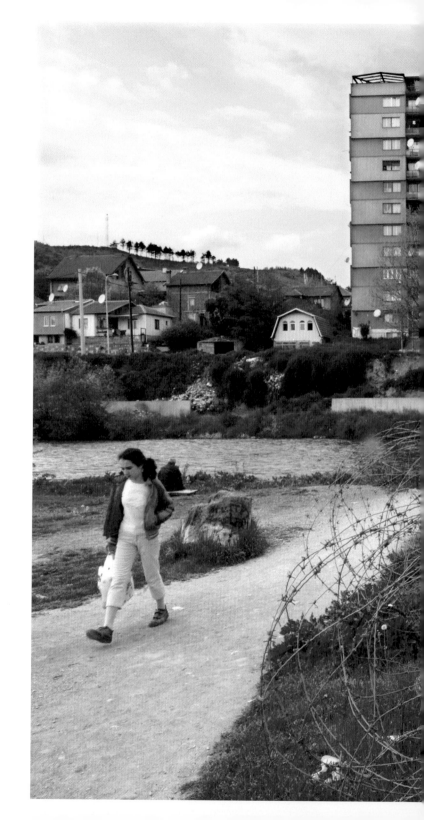

The Three Towers
was 'a place of open
doors' before the war,
according to Sanije.
Today the Ibër/Ibar
river marks a *de facto*
border between
Albanians and Serbs.

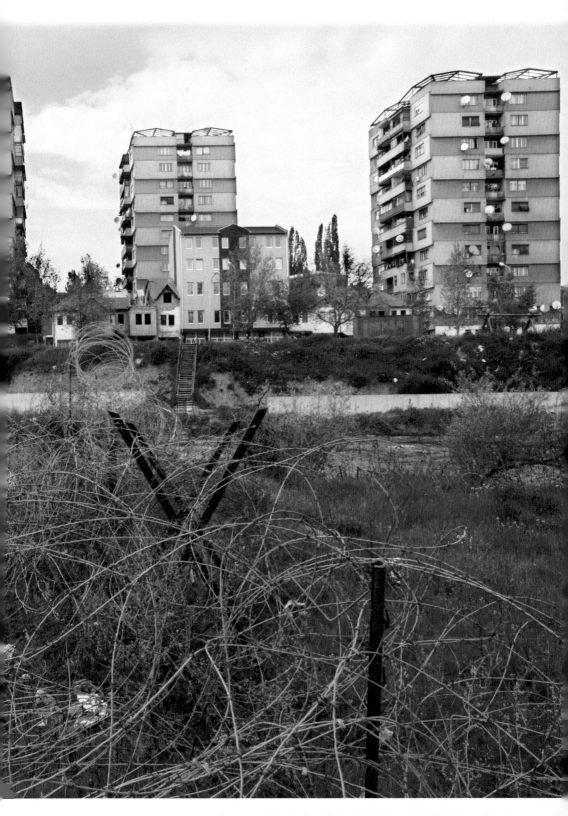

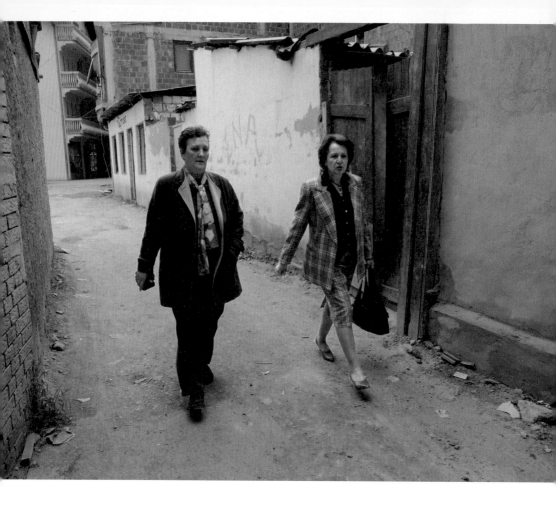

In Mitrovica there
lives at least one man
who knows Bekim's
fate, as well as where
his body might be
found. 'That's my
former neighbour,
the man in the mask
who took them away,'
said Sanije.

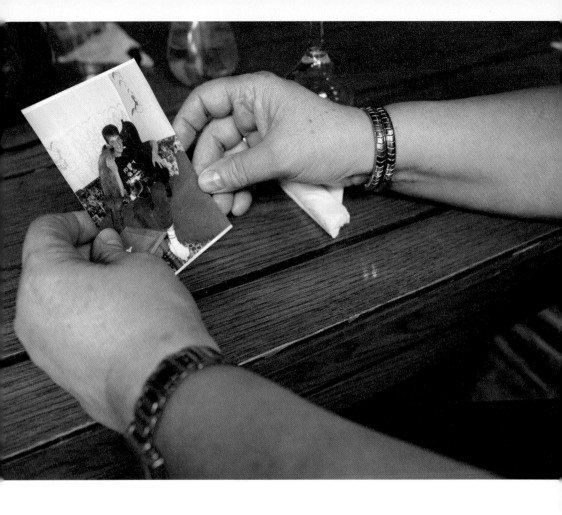

Bekim Recaj was
abducted from his
home – along with
his two uncles – on
the day that peace
was declared in
Kosovo.

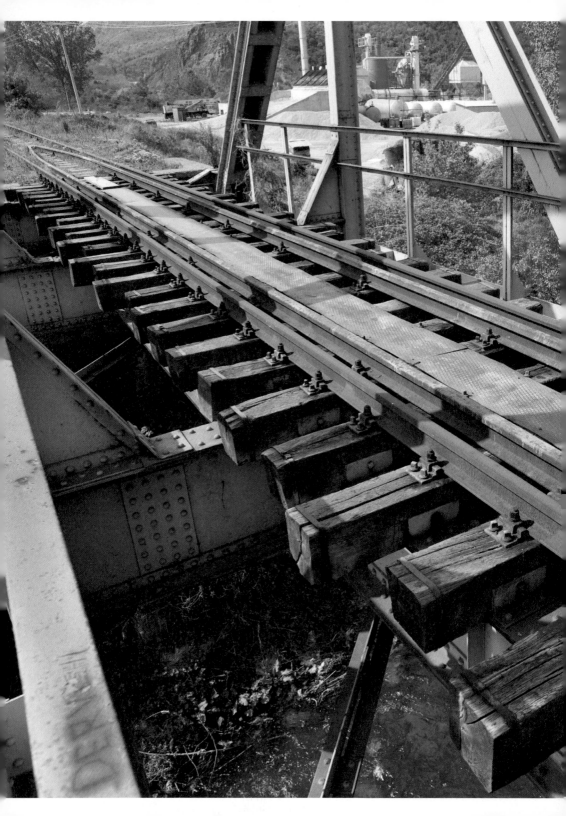

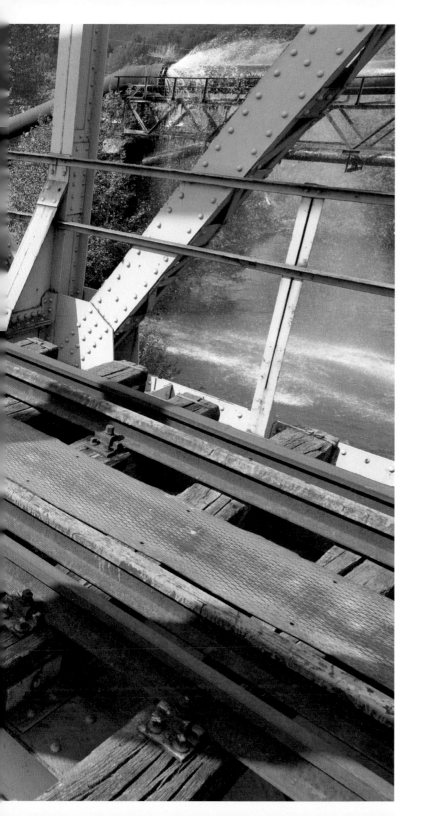

Bekim Recaj, his two
uncles and 13 neigh-
bours from the Three
Towers apartments
were ordered to
jump into the Ibër/
Ibar river near to the
railway bridge. The
police then began to
shoot at them.

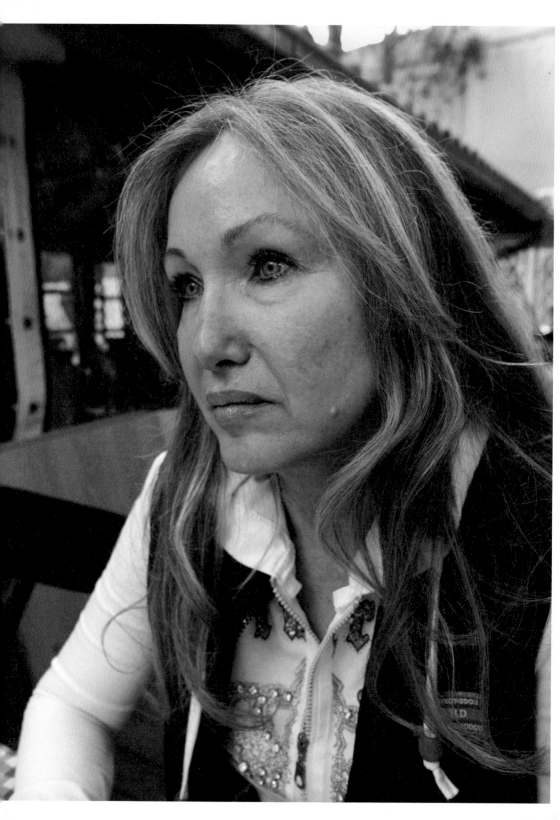

[Rade Budimir]

'We met on holiday in Russia,' said Olja Budimir, her pale blue eyes hidden behind designer sunglasses. Under the trees dappled sunlight flickered across her face. 'Rade was the tour guide. We were dancing our first dance – I remember he moved so beautifully – when he was called away to deal with another tourist. That half-dance was like our life to come, never to be completed.'

On their return to the Balkans Olja and Rade started dating each other. One summer evening they were walking around the old Turkish Kalemegdan fortress in Belgrade. Music rose up from a nearby restaurant and suddenly they were waltzing along the battlements.

'Rade told me that he knew I'd be his wife one day,' she said, the shifting shadows playing tricks with her expression. 'I just jumped into his life.'

Rade Budimir was an energetic and social fiftysomething, a lover of nights on the town and old Serbian folksongs, a director of the Putnik Travel Agency in Pristina. After they married, he and Olja travelled together to France, Italy, Germany and Greece. In Cyprus he took off his tie and jacket to dance the kalamatianos. In Halkidiki they went for long happy walks along the Aegean coast.

'We kept travelling as if nothing was going to happen,' Olja said, her lips lifting into a pouting smile.

Their trips ended when war came to Kosovo. She and Rade stayed at home in Pristina throughout the fighting and bombing, sheltering Albanian neighbours, waiting for the conflict to pass. To them, like most Serbs, Kosovo was an integral part of their country. 'We lived in Serbia and Serbia would protect us.'

But when Serbian forces finally withdrew from the disputed territory, Pristina became 'a slaughterhouse'. Albanian vigilante

groups embarked on a swathe of bloody revenge killings.

'I saw cars full of blood. I heard shooting and crying. If you were not there you would not believe what was happening,' she recalled, her lips curling in an involuntary twist.

The roads were deadly dangerous – convoys had been ambushed and a bus blown up – but Rade and Olja decided to try to escape from Kosovo with her family.

'We had to try our luck. We loaded the cars quickly, before any Albanians could attack us. Then just as we were about to leave Rade said he wasn't coming. My heart seemed to stop beating in my chest. All my relatives were in the cars. I was one of the drivers. I had no choice but to go.'

Olja and her family fled, taking refuge in a farmhouse just outside Kosovo. While nursing her invalid father, Olja rang Rade at home. 'He told me that the troubles would be over in a few days. He simply wanted to get on with life.' The call ended with their usual teasing double entendre. 'It's a miracle that I love you,' he said.

Three weeks later Rade failed to arrive in Belgrade for a business meeting. In Pristina Olja's brother – who had stayed behind in the city – found four Albanians living in their apartment. The strangers had changed the door lock and, when he asked to see the old lock, he found Rade's key in it. His suspicion aroused, he asked KFOR, whose headquarters were across the road, to intervene. The NATO soldiers took away the four men only 'to let them go out of their back door'.

Olja was 'in complete madness'. She rang hospitals, churches and morgues as well as her Serb and Albanian friends. A month later she moved alone to Belgrade to hound government ministries as well as the ICRC and Serbian Red Cross. She was given a small hotel room by Rade's travel agency for one night. With no other place to stay it became her home for most of the next four years.

'Always there were rumours,' she said. 'One morning I would hear that he was alive in a prison camp, the next that he was dead.' An Albanian acquaintance told her from Pristina, 'Rade will always be my friend, in this world and in the next one.' She tracked every rumour back to its source, calling the friend who had heard it from a cousin who had claimed to have seen Rade. She toiled with a fanatical meticulousness, refusing to 'sit at home and cry. My objective was to find him, or at least his remains. I had to prevent dogs from carrying away his bones, to stop him from being just another statistic.'

At the same time Olja worked for the Family Association of Missing and Kidnapped Persons from Kosovo. 'The first evening I stood in a corner, crying behind my glasses. I heard heartbreaking stories about mothers who had lost their sons, daughters who had lost their parents. I thought, I have only lost my husband.' Olja's humility and determination made her a tireless advocate for the association, and she rose to the position of Co-ordinator.

Then one year after his disappearance Olja went to an exhibition of photographs of personal belongings found on unidentified exhumed bodies. 'I saw hundreds of pictures of jeans, shirts, skirts. They all looked the same. Halfway through the exhibition I almost stopped looking. Suddenly I recognised the dark blue suede shoes we'd bought together in Greece.'

Later she was shown the shoes and clothes themselves. 'I recognised the jacket I'd washed and ironed. I found one of his hairs on the shirt.' She had brought with her a copy of Rade's dental records to confirm his identity. Only then did she learn that no head had been found. The body had been decapitated.

No one knew who had killed or buried him, nor what had become of the four Albanian strangers.

Even with a DNA match, Olja had difficulty accepting that the headless corpse with broken arms could be her vibrant, dancing Rade. His body was brought from Pristina to the border in a cheap wooden coffin held together by packing tape. There he was transferred into an ornate coffin she had brought from Belgrade. UN soldiers in their blue helmets, who had failed to protect him in life, stood guard as the blue coffin lining was folded over the white body bag.

'I lost my husband, my love, my chance to have children,' said Olja. 'I ached like a wounded, wild animal yet I held my head high, proudly and with a smile on my face, without really knowing why.' Against all the odds she found the courage to move on with her life. 'But there was no way I would be forced to wear a headscarf,' she went on, the music of her voice revealing a flint hard edge. 'My suffering was no less because I chose to wear a yellow dress. Time and time again I've had to explain my understanding of mourning. External appearances do not indicate the depth of emotion. I chose to fight by remaining the way I was in the past. Otherwise I'd have killed myself.'

Olja sold the old Pristina apartment and bought a smaller place in Belgrade. She found a job, joined a trekking club and began to travel again. 'I cried so much on my first holiday, but I knew I simply had to work through it. I've now trekked in Turkey and Europe, and that sort of travel suits me; I can be with the group or walk alone as the mood takes me.'

As day turned to evening Olja took off her dark glasses and looked out through the woods. 'My life belongs only to myself now. I still love Rade but I cannot say that I will remain alone forever. Everything is possible in life.'

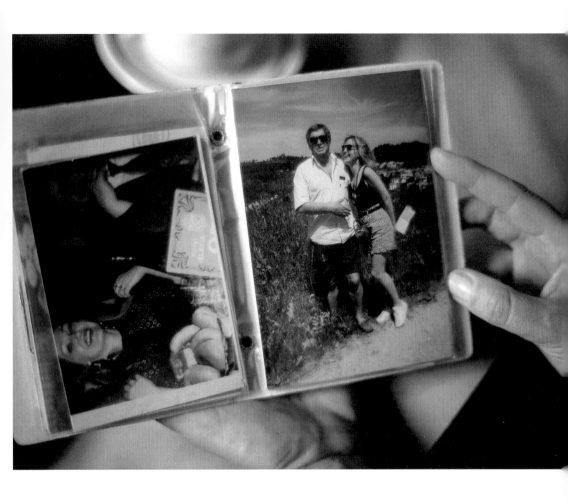

Olja and Rade met on
holiday and travelled
together to a dozen
countries before his
murder.

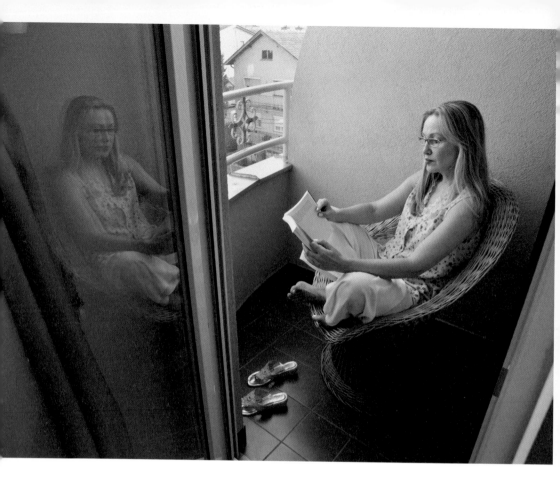

'What kind of a mind
assumes the right
to inflict pain on
others and take away
a life?' asked Olja,
who now lives alone
in Belgrade. 'By mur-
dering one family
member, all those
he belonged with are
murdered too.'

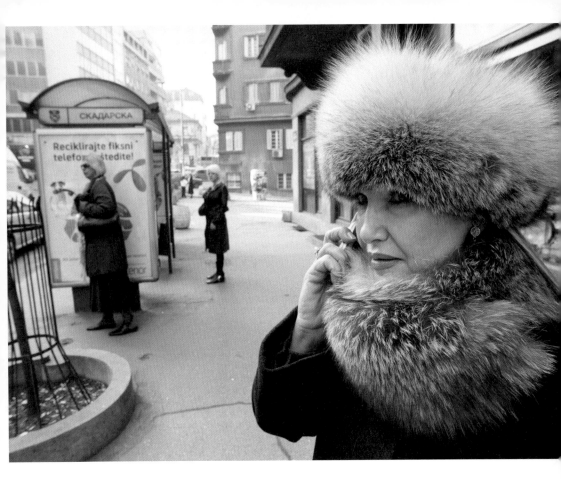

Olja refuses to hide
herself away, to dress
in mourning black,
to claim that her suf-
fering is greater than
another's suffering.
'External appearances
do not indicate the
depth of emotion,'
she said.

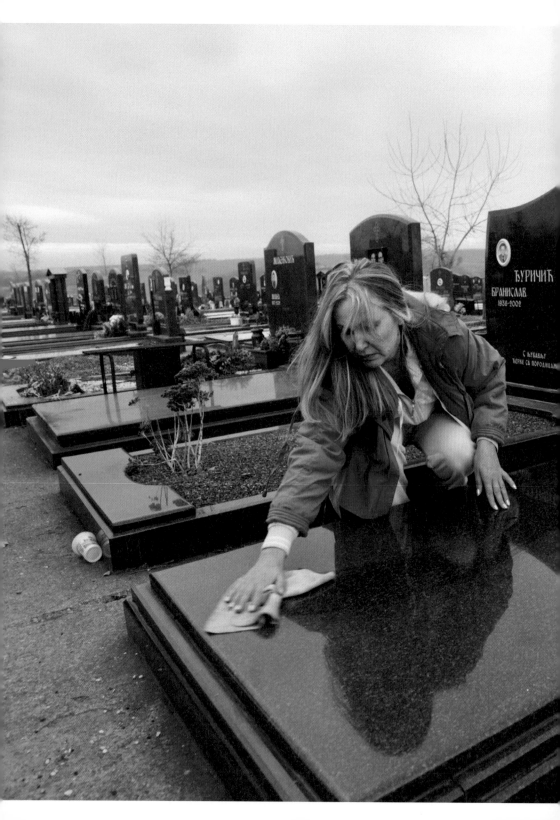

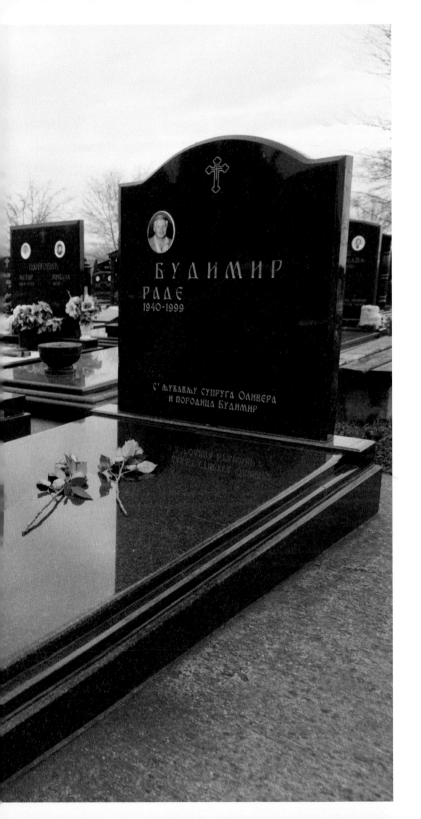

БУДИМИР
РАДЕ
1940-1999

С' ЉУБАВЉУ СУПРУГА ОЛИВЕРА
И ПОРОДИЦА БУДИМИР

Initially Rade's headless body was interred in Pristina's Dragodan cemetery as Unknown JA 041/008. Later his remains were exhumed, identified and reburied in Belgrade. 'The only place I feel good is at the grave of my Rade,' said Olja. 'It is all I really have now.'

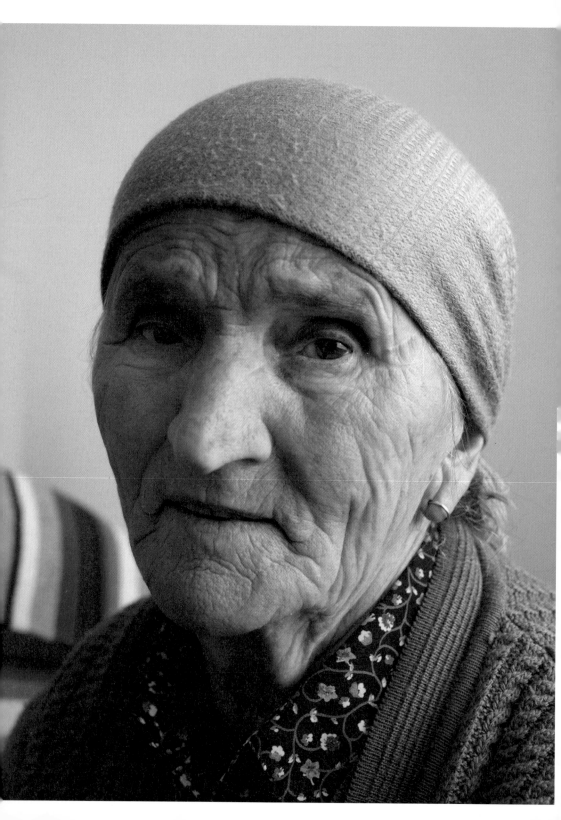

   [Nasuf 'John' Berisha]

In years gone by Nexhmedin Nasuf Berisha sat on his blanket
beneath the cherry trees, gazing down the gently sloping valley
toward the Sitnica river. He called out his friendly, tuneless greeting
to everyone who visited the farm, everyone that is but the chickens.
He hated the chickens because they stole his bread. He loved his
mother's warm bread and always seemed to have a piece of it in his
hand. Once the rooster tried to take it from him and Nasuf seized it
by its neck. The rooster started pecking and tearing at Nasuf's arms
until his brother Fetah grabbed the bird and chopped off its head.
   'He was the most beautiful of all my babies,' said Sela Berisha,
his petite 81-year-old mother. 'I was always with him. I never hid
him away.'
   Nasuf had been born with Down's syndrome, a chromosomal
disorder that impairs cognitive ability. He couldn't walk until he
was seven years old. His vocabulary never expanded beyond a dozen
words: Nana, Papa, water, warm bread. Yet he was a happy child,
inventing nonsensical rhymes from people's names, growing into
a vast, gentle giant who sat Buddha-like on the grass or his trailer,
comforted by his family's love, unconcerned by the approach of war.
   In the summer of 1998 four Serbian armed personnel carriers
took up position in a nearby pinewood and idly began shelling
Bivolak, the Berishas' village outside Vushtri. Bullets whizzed over
Nasuf's head as his trailer was hitched onto the tractor and carried to safety in the forested Qiqavica hills. The next day the family
returned to the farm. The pattern was repeated every week until
September when masked paramilitaries evicted the villagers and
burnt down their houses. Nasuf and ten members of his family

were bullied from one place to another, finally finding refuge in a tiny room in Pristina. Most of them wintered there, Nasuf's father Shefqet trekking out to the land whenever possible to care for the animals. On one of those journeys he didn't return.

On that same spring day, the police ordered the family out of their room. Serbian forces inside Kosovo had embarked on a campaign of ethnic cleansing, using artillery to reduce entire villages to rubble, forcing hundreds of thousands of Kosovo Albanians to flee for their lives.

On Pristina's streets Nasuf's family confronted a scene of terrifying brutality. Masked 'security forces' herded as many as ten thousand ethnic Albanians towards the train station, arbitrarily pulling individuals from the columns, threatening to shoot them unless paid a ransom. Around midnight the refugees were packed onto filthy carriages. Nasuf was hoisted in through a window. No one knew their destination and the fear of death camps haunted their minds. Only Nasuf, who had always loved to travel, was happy.

At dawn the train reached the Macedonian border. The police seized the refugees' documents and the last of their money and ordered them across the frontier. The family were forced to separate, leaving Nasuf and his mother in the care of her 14-year-old grandson Valon.

Valon scoured the neighbourhood for a wheelbarrow. He found a child's pram but it collapsed when Nasuf was lowered into it. He and Sela, aged 72 at the time, tried to drag Nasuf along the now-deserted road. At that moment two young aid workers appeared with a stretcher. They offered to carry Nasuf to safety.

'I remember his big belly wobbling as they carried him away,' said Sela.

Nasuf was taken to a medical facility set up between the two

countries by the International Catholic Migration Commission.
One of the stretcher-bearers said, 'You go. We'll look after him.'
In their fear and exhaustion, in the rush and shouting of soldiers,
no one thought to write down Nasuf's name.

Sela and Valon managed to find the rest of their family in the
vast throng. But the Macedonian guards would not let them go
back across the border. Valon's last sight of Nasuf was of him sitting
outside a tent in no-man's-land, smiling up at the sun.

After three days in the open, with little water and no food, the
rain began. By the fourth day the camp was a stinking quagmire.
The thousands of refugees were loaded onto Macedonian trains –
Sela lost her shoes in the mud – and shipped away from the frontier.

In Kosovo the NATO bombing finally forced the Serbian forces to
withdraw. KFOR replaced the Yugoslav structures, prompting the
return of refugees. Fetah – who had killed the chicken – came back
to Bivolak, followed by the family. He registered as missing his
father, his uncle and his brother Nasuf. One month later a neighbour told him to go to Te Furra, a hill which had served as a Serbian
observation post during the war.

'When I came near there was such a strong smell,' said Fetah, a
dignified and reserved 60-year-old. 'In one small area I saw deep
tracks where a tank had been driven around and around. In the
ruts I found shards of bone, a burnt shoe and a part-buried piece
of a shirt. I pulled it out of the earth, washed it and showed it to my
mother, Sela. She said, "That is your father's shirt."'

With a pick and shovel Fetah unearthed the crushed remains of
his father and his missing uncle, trying to sort and reassemble their
scorched skeletons and possessions on the hilltop.

'Every bone, even the skulls, were broken,' he said. 'But there

was no crying. Death is death. Our concern was more with Nasuf.'

Fetah opened searches with a local NGO, the ICRC, the IOM and the UNHCR as well as the French police, then in charge of security in Bivolak. With the help of the Red Cross, young Valon even travelled back to Macedonia for ten days. But no trace of Nasuf could be found.

At the border Nasuf, unable to say his name, had been renamed 'John' by a Macedonian aid worker. He had sat in a wheelchair for the first time in his life (the family had never been able to afford one). After the evacuation of the refugees, he was transferred by the Macedonian Red Cross to an asylum in distant Demir Hisar. There he lived for the last year of his life, dying a few weeks before the link was established back to his family. At the asylum there were no cherry trees. He didn't eat freshly baked bread. Again and again he called out for his mother. 'How did he die?' a nurse at the asylum was asked later. 'He died of a broken heart.'

At Bivolak a magpie landed on the garage pocked with bullet holes. A cuckoo called from the Qiqavica hills. Chickens pecked at the base of the electricity pylons. In the distance a KFOR Apache helicopter buzzed above the cooling tower of the Kosovo 'B' power plant.

'There are people who say that one forgets over time,' said Sela. 'But my memory of Nasuf is so fresh.' She paused for a moment. 'I was relieved when I learnt that he had been buried. But it would mean so much to me to have his remains back. It would be like bringing him back to me alive.'

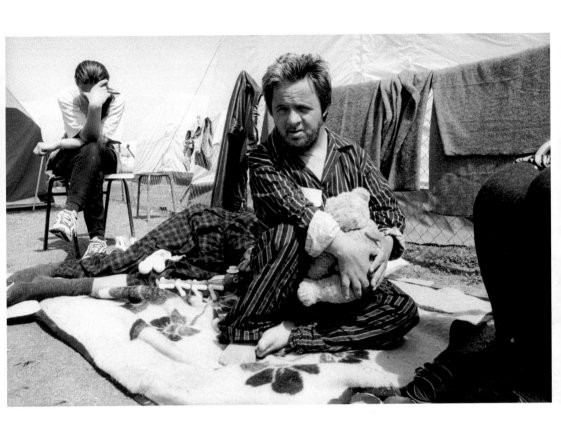

Until the moment he
was left on the Mace-
donian border, Nasuf
had never been sepa-
rated from the family.
Rather than return
him to Kosovo, he
was transferred to
an asylum in distant
Demir Hisar where
– lost and unable to
speak – he died of a
broken heart.

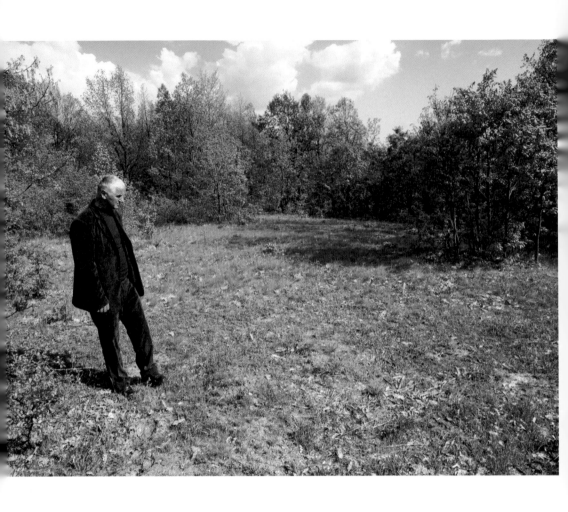

Nasuf's brother
Fetah stares at the
spot near their home
where he found
the crushed bodies
of their father and
uncle. 'Every bone,
even the skulls, were
broken,' he said.

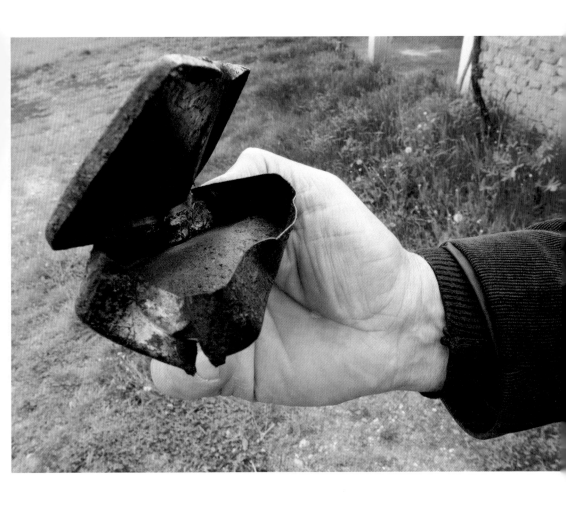

Among the shards
of bone and burnt
clothing, Fetah
found their uncle's
tobacco tin, pierced
by a bullet and
crushed by a tank.

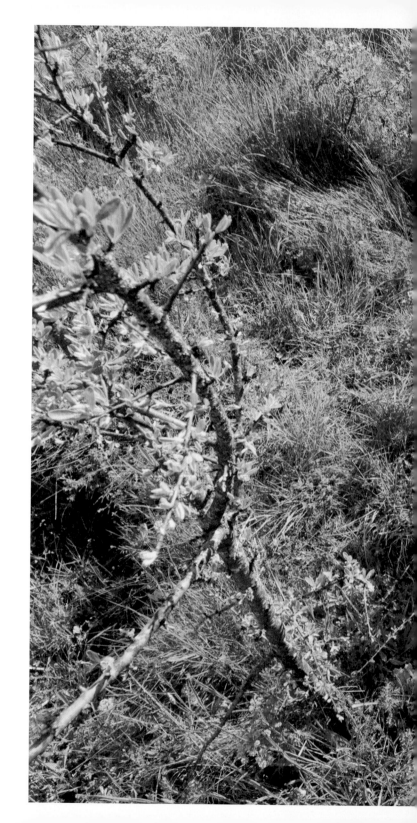

Nasuf's unmarked grave near the Macedonian asylum. To this day his exhumation and return to Kosovo has not been possible.

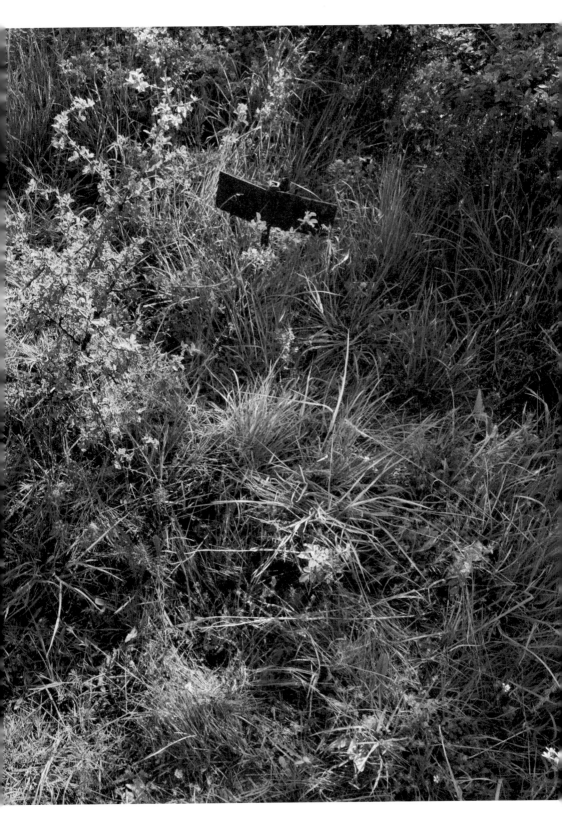

In conflicts people disappear leaving no trace. The stories told in *Missing Lives* illustrate some of the deepest scars of war: the loss of loved ones without knowing their fate, and the inability to let the dead rest with dignity. They also show that the lives lost are those of the bereaved as much as the deceased.

Not knowing the whereabouts of a husband or wife, a son or daughter, a father or mother prolongs the suffering. Only by meeting and listening to these families does one begin to understand the depth of their torment.

The fate of more than half of the persons reported missing during the successive conflicts in the former Yugoslavia has been established. Thousands of human remains were found and handed over to their families. This is a positive result when one looks at the very low rate of resolutions from the conflicts in Iraq, Guatemala or Chechnya. Three reasons explain why the search for missing persons has been relatively successful in the Western Balkans. First, the families could rapidly report their missing relatives to the Red Cross and other international bodies who had maintained an extensive field presence during the war. Second, DNA technology made significant progress during the past decade, increasing greatly the possibilities for positive identification of anonymous human remains. Third, the issue of the missing was placed high on the agenda of the international community, both by putting pressure on former warring parties to provide answers to the families, and by funding the slow and expensive process of identifying human remains found in gravesites across the region.

Over the past years, several international and national key players in each country of the Balkans have helped families and their

associations in numerous ways. Their work also helped to keep the
issue of missing persons and the needs of the families in the region
under the spotlight of attention of the local governments and of
the international community.

However, it is clear that much more remains to be done. It is
simply unacceptable that the fate of more than 15,000 persons
remains unknown and that their families continue to endure such
suffering. Tens of thousands of relatives cannot lay their emotions
to rest and this continues to adversely affect peace and reconciliation throughout the region. Efforts must focus on providing
answers and information on the missing. They must also focus on
helping families address their pressing legal, economic and social
needs.

Under international humanitarian law, states party to the
Geneva Conventions are primarily accountable to the victims of
armed conflicts. They have an obligation to provide answers to families on the whereabouts of people who disappeared in the territo-
ries under their control during the conflict. To fulfil this obligation,
states in the former Yugoslavia must do more. First, they have to
initiate an extensive search for information on the fate of missing
persons, including through data related to potential gravesites or
to transfers of human remains that could have taken place during
or immediately after the conflict. Second, they must increase the
budgets they allocate to their national commissions in order to
speed up the exhumation and identification process. Third and perhaps most difficult, governments in the Western Balkans have to
start exchanging information unconditionally on the whereabouts
of missing persons.

Common Article 1 of the four Geneva Conventions demands that
signatory states undertake to respect and to ensure respect for the

168

Conventions in all circumstances. Based on this, the ICRC urges governments in the Western Balkans, as well as others who have a stake in the region, to intensify their efforts towards bringing answers to families of the missing.

Behind the many statistics and statements, there are individual men, women and children whose lives were torn apart by untold violence. It is a fundamental issue of dignity that the thousands of affected families receive news and support. It remains as urgent as ever to elucidate the fate of their missing loved ones.

Pierre Krähenbühl
Director of Operations
International Committee of the Red Cross

The Long Search

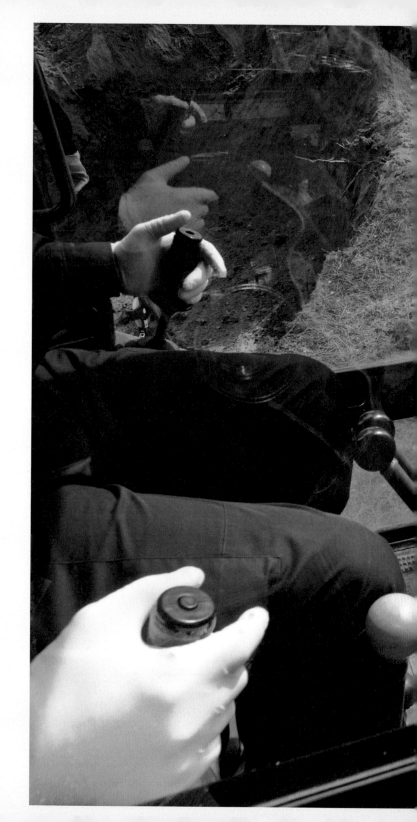

Exhumations
continue across
the Balkans.

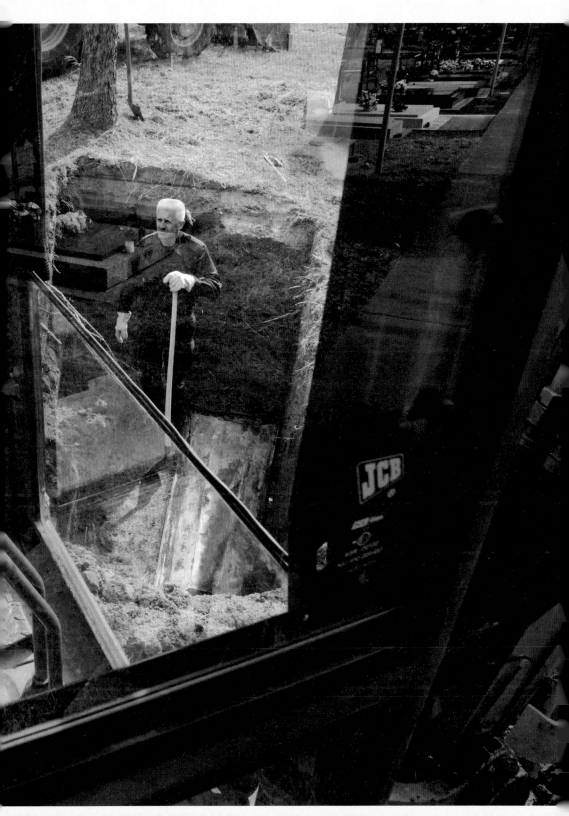

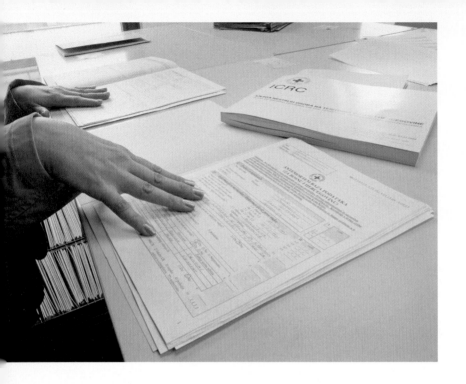

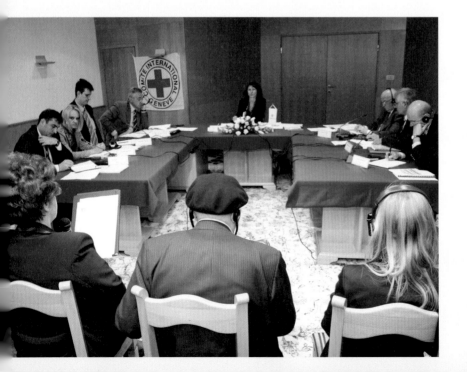

above:
When reporting
a disappearance,
families complete
a Tracing Request
and provide ante-
mortem data. Lists
of the missing are
regularly updated
and published
throughout the
region.

left:
Chaired by the
ICRC, the Working
Group on Persons
Unaccounted for
in Kosovo brings
together former
warring parties to
exchange informa-
tion on the fate of
missing persons.
In 2004 over 3,000
people were still
missing as a result
of the conflict in
Kosovo. Five years
later that number
had been reduced to
1,869. (photograph
by Bozidar Petrovic)

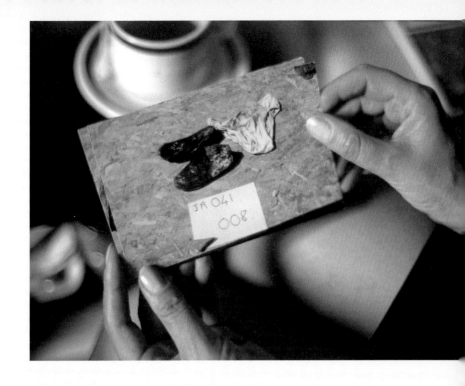

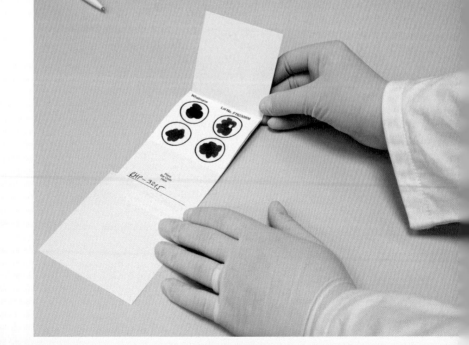

above:
Photographs of personal items recovered from graves are published in Books of Belongings.

right:
By matching DNA from bone and blood samples, the dead can be linked to living blood relatives.

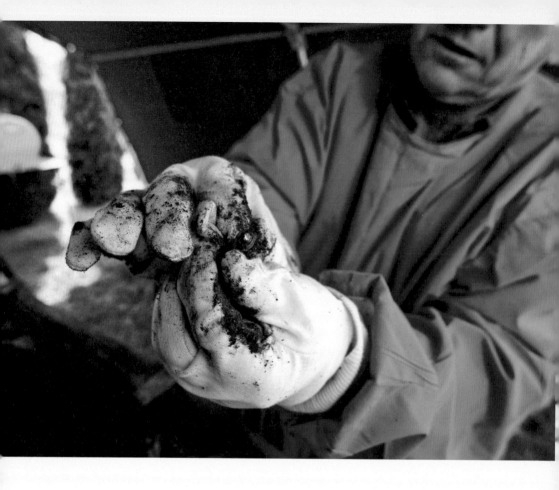

Unearthed personal
items, such as an
engagement ring,
can contribute to
identification.

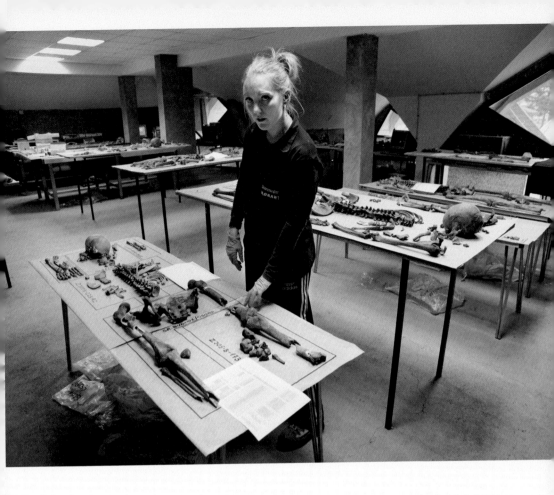

ICMP anthropolo-
gists reassemble
the disarticulated
remains of victims
from – in some
cases – as many as
four different graves.
Burnt bones are
often too damaged
to contain DNA.

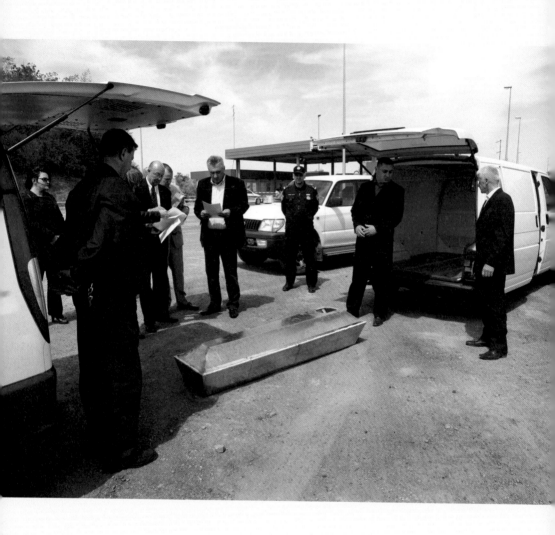

Across the region
officials exchange
identified bodies at
border crossings.

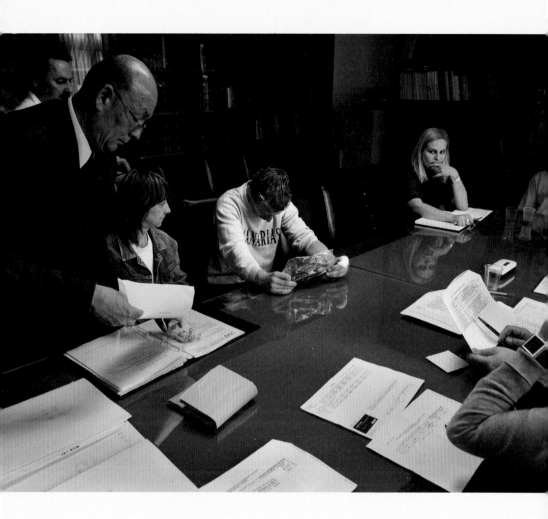

Commissions on missing persons invite families for identification sessions during which they receive DNA and death certificates. The remains are then prepared and handed over for burial.

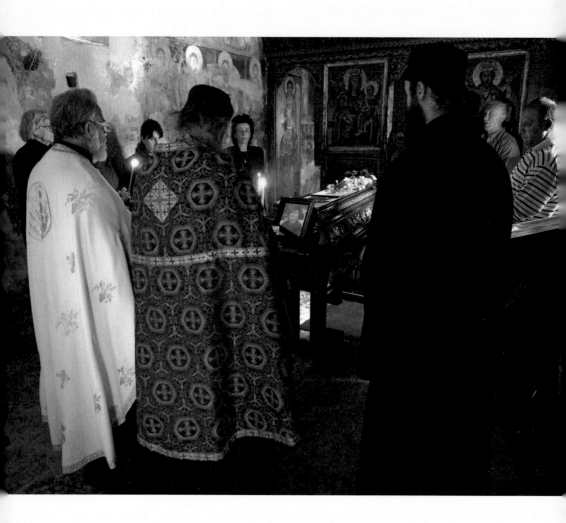

above and right:
The burial of people
who went missing
years ago remains a
common occurrence
in the Balkans.

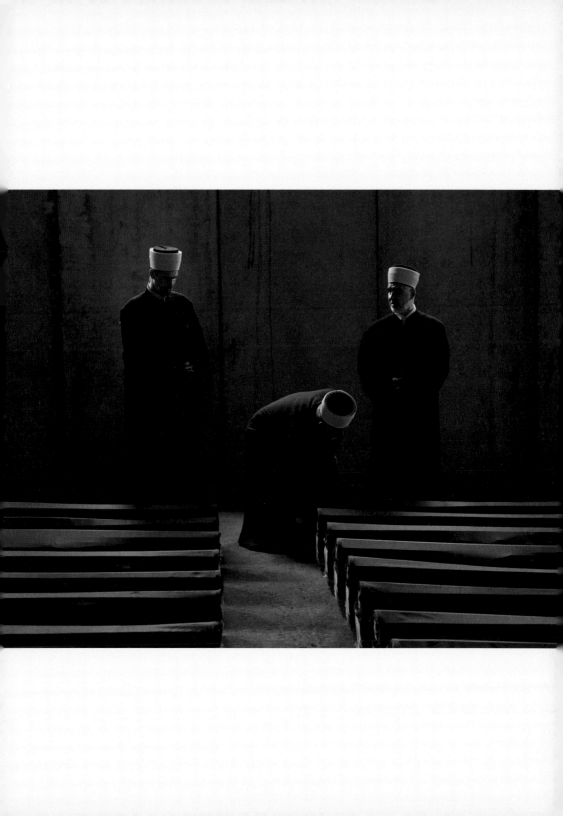

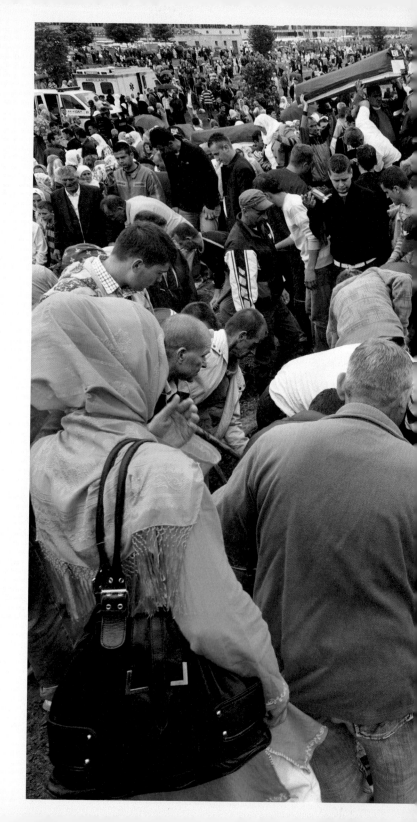

Every year in
Srebrenica, a
collective burial
is organised for
hundreds of
newly-identified
human remains.

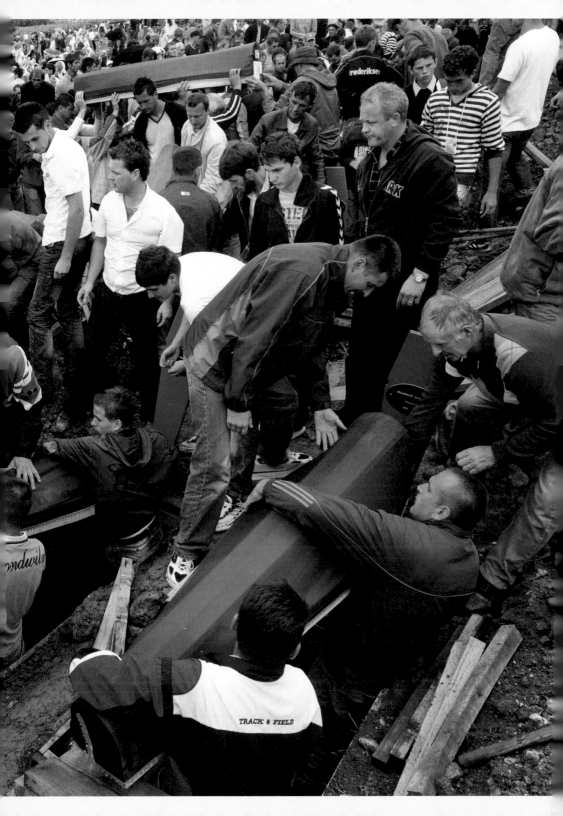

Nick Danziger is an artist, travel writer, photographer and film-maker. Awarded a Winston Churchill Memorial Fellowship in 1982, he traced ancient trade routes from Turkey to China, documenting his adventures in *Danziger's Travels*, the first of many bestselling books. In 1991 he made his first documentary, *War, Lives and Videotape*, about children abandoned in an Afghan mental asylum, which won the Prix Italia for best television documentary. His photographic work is held in museum collections worldwide and earned him the Royal Geographical Society's Ness Award in recognition of raising public understanding of contemporary social, political and environmental issues. His 'mirror' image of Tony Blair and George W. Bush won the World Press Photo award. 'It's no exaggeration to say that Nick Danziger is one of the finest photojournalists this country has ever produced,' wrote *Digital Camera*. 'He's a naturally gifted visual storyteller.' In 2007 he was awarded an Honorary Fellowship by the Royal Photographic Society.

Rory MacLean's seven books, including UK bestsellers *Stalin's Nose* and *Under the Dragon*, have challenged and invigorated travel writing, and according to the late John Fowles are among works that 'marvellously explain why literature still lives'. During his research journeys, MacLean walked through the newly-opened Berlin Wall, met Aung San Suu Kyi in Rangoon and interviewed Pashtun elders at the Kacha Garhi refugee camp after the destruction of the World Trade Center. His books have won awards from the Canada Council and the Arts Council of England, were shortlisted for the Thomas Cook Travel Book Prize and nominated for the International IMPAC Dublin Literary award. He is a Fellow of the Royal Society of Literature and an active member of EnglishPEN. He has written and presented over 50 programmes for BBC radio and worked on movies with David Bowie, Marlene Dietrich and Ken Russell. Born in Canada and resident for many years in Britain, he now lives with his family in Berlin.